£10.50

FLOWERS & PLANTS in EMBROIDERY

VALERIE
CAMPBELL-HARDING

FLOWERS & PLANTS in EMBROIDERY

B.T. Batsford Ltd
London

ISBN 0 7134 1313 1

Typeset by Servis Filmsetting Ltd, Manchester
and printed in Great Britain by
Courier International Ltd
Tiptree, Essex
for the publishers
B.T. Batsford Ltd
4 Fitzhardinge Street
London W1H 0AH

ACKNOWLEDGEMENT

I would like to thank the following people for
their help: all the friends and students who
allowed me to use their drawings or to
photograph their work to illustrate this book;
Melvyn Farley who developed my films and
printed the photographs; J.&P. Coats who
very kindly sent me some embroidery threads
for stitching some of the samples and
embroideries. In particular, many thanks to
Jan Messent who did some drawings espe-
cially for me.

AUTHOR'S NOTE

This book does not include detailed descrip-
tions of methods and techniques, as it is
aimed at the many embroiderers who already
have some knowledge of these. There are
many other good books available which cover all aspects of embroidery.

CONTENTS

1 *Drawing by Jan Messent from a sixteenth-century herbal.*

ONE

LOOKING FOR PATTERN IN FLOWERS & PLANTS

For hundreds of years, embroiderers have looked to flowers and plants for inspiration, and they are still doing so. Nature is a rich source of pattern, colour and texture, and once you begin looking at markings on leaves, the way the colours blend in the petal of a flower, or the shape of a seedhead, you will find a never-ending source of ideas. It is sometimes useful to take photographs, but really you must draw to learn about the subject; and having spent some time on the drawing, you will remember forever what you have been looking at. You can also take rubbings, which is a very quick way of note-taking, but cannot be used on everything. It is also worth looking at how flowers and plants have been treated by other artists and craftsmen, both recently and in the past.

Having collected some reference material, you will find that some aspects of the subject interest you more than others; you will gradually narrow your horizons, and ways of using some of the material you have collected will begin to emerge. Then you begin to design – which only means planning what you are going to embroider, and on what. The result may be something to wear, something to decorate your house, or something for an exhibition. The practical aspects of, say, a cushion which will receive hard wear, or a lampshade through which the light must shine, may suggest certain techniques or types of stitchery to be used, so consider these aspects carefully. The next consideration is the shape of the article, as the design must complement it. Then you must consider the colour scheme – will you use the realistic colours of the original, or will you choose an imaginative scheme that is quite unrealistic? It is always worth doing your design on paper in at least two different colourways to see the difference.

This book begins with a section on things to look at and ways to collect the information. The following chapters suggest ways of designing based on some of the drawings and photographs, with suggestions of how to carry them out in embroidery, and what to do with them. Embroidery is affected by fashion just as much as clothes are, so I have tended to put suggestions into words, rather than too many drawings. If you are thinking of embroidery on household articles or clothes, then look at up-to-date magazines and adapt some of your ideas to the current shapes and patterns.

2 *Pencil sketch of a vine growing against a wall, by Christine Cooke. She has added notes to remind her of details of colour and lighting when she uses the sketch in the future. No drawing can give all the necessary information, so do not hesitate to make all the notes you will need.*

3 *Pencil drawing of some plants in pots, by Christine Cooke. Again, she has made notes to remind her of the colours, and the fact that the plants are growing against a white wall and sitting on paving stones. She gives an extremely good indication of the different textures of the plants, and her style is very suggestive of stitchery.*

8

4 *A line drawing of monstera leaves, drawn from a gardening magazine. Here it is the shapes that are important, and the spaces between the stems.*

5 *A pen drawing of a cactus, by Anne Hazlewood. She is concerned with the fleshy quality of the leaves, and the shapes of them. No single drawing can show everything, so consider carefully what it is that appeals to you.*

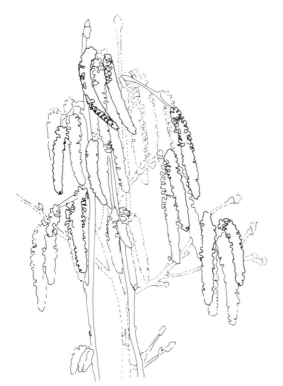

6 *A drawing from a design by Charles Rennie Mackintosh on a greetings card. It shows lambs' tails on a hazel tree, and the original was done in soft water colour with slightly deeper lines to give definition. My drawing uses three different sizes of pen to give different thicknesses of line and so a feeling of depth, and suggests frilled edges of fabric and machine embroidery.*

7 *(Below) A panel by Mary Day of trees, fields and bushes in the foreground. Lines were drawn on the silk fabric with gold gutta (which acts as a resist to stop the paint from running), then silk paints were used to colour in the different areas. The panel is quilted using whip stitch on the sewing machine.*

8 *(Opposite) A collection of drawings of trees, some symbolic, some stylized and some realistic.*
(a) These are from Japanese trade marks.
(b) A stylized tree with bare, winter branches.
(c) A real tree, but simplified to show the shapes and dark shadows.
(d) Trees from Czechoslovakian paper cuts.

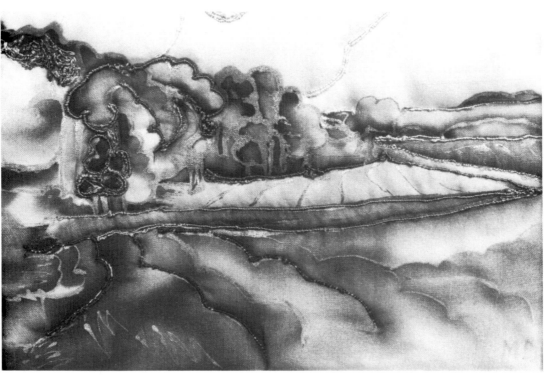

(a)

(b)

(c)

(d)

9 *Groups of leaves, either one plant or several, can show an enormous variation in shape, texture, and direction of growth.*

10 *The furriness of these leaves completely hides the pattern of the veins, and makes them seem very thick. The direction of the hairs would make the stitching of these leaves fairly simple, using little straight stitches. Alternatively they could be made from a fabric such as velvet, stiffened with PVA (a white, washable glue) and moulded to give wavy edges.*

11 *Rubbings can record texture and pattern very quickly. Stretch a piece of thin paper over a surface. Holding the paper firmly so that is does not slip, rub a wax crayon, or the side of a pencil, over the paper (exactly as if you were doing a brass rubbing), and the pattern will emerge. It is even more effective if you use a rainbow- or multi-coloured crayon or pencil. This is a rubbing of a Javanese printing block.*

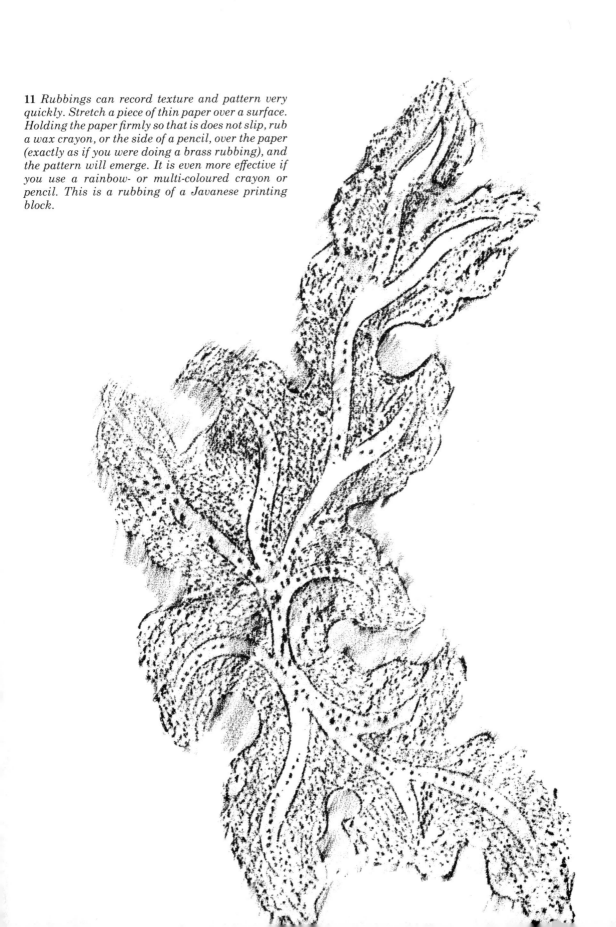

12 *A drawing of hanging leaves, mainly in pen, but one in pencil to show the different effect. I have used these leaves in a great many patterns and borders, in different embroideries, so have had real value from one drawing session. Apart from the fact that drawing is a learning process, one drawing can be used repeatedly for different designs in different styles and different techniques.*

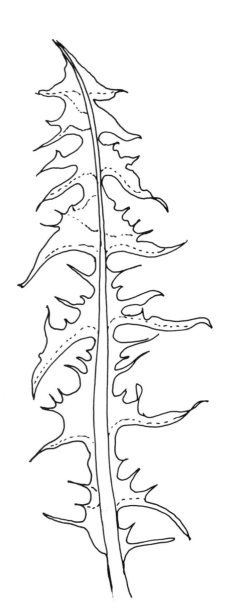

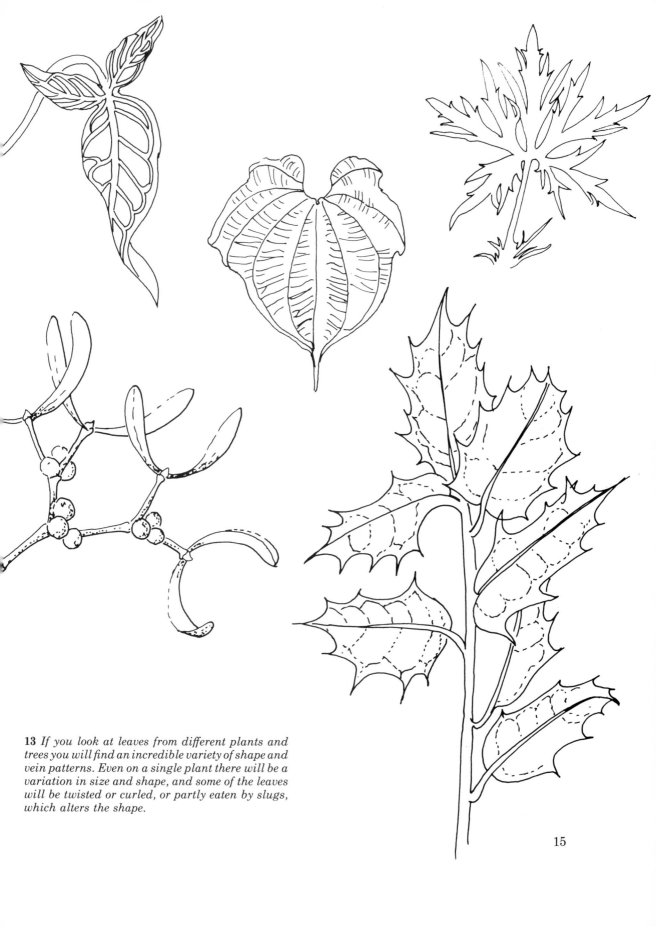

13 *If you look at leaves from different plants and trees you will find an incredible variety of shape and vein patterns. Even on a single plant there will be a variation in size and shape, and some of the leaves will be twisted or curled, or partly eaten by slugs, which alters the shape.*

15

14 (Opposite) *Massed leaves growing at different angles and in different directions can suggest texture if looked at from a distance, or all-over patterns if seen from closer to. Here the shadows, the cream edges of some of the leaves, and the vein lines, are a rich source of pattern.*

15 *Dead leaves, hanging from their stems, give quite a different look to what we usually consider to be flat shapes. Here they have curled up to make three-dimensional enclosed forms. Pieces of embroidery could be curled up in the same way and then applied to a background fabric.*

16 *These massed yucca flowers, photographed in France, are a pale creamy colour. The plant has a single stem with an incredible number of flowers growing on it for most of its length.*

17 *(a) A drawing of a painting of arum lilies by Van Gogh. His style of painting is very suggestive of stitchery.*
(b) A delicate pen drawing of marsh mallow flowers by Jan Messent, showing the contrast between buds, fully opened flowers and leaves.

(b)

(a)

18 *Single and clustered flowers suggest different approaches to design. The fragile, frilled petals of a poppy have a quality that can be interpreted in transparent fabrics, while the hydrangea is more easily interpreted in appliqué or stitchery.*

19 *A box by Wendy Williams with velvet pansies and stems made from rouleaux.*

(a)

(b)

(c)

(d)

20 *Four very stylized flowers from other periods and countries.*
(a) Honeysuckle from a William Morris printed fabric.
(b) Chrysanthemum from a Japanese woven brocade.
(c) A Tiffany glass plate.
(d) Camellia from a Chinese embroidery design. This would probably have been worked in Pekin knots or satin stitch.

21

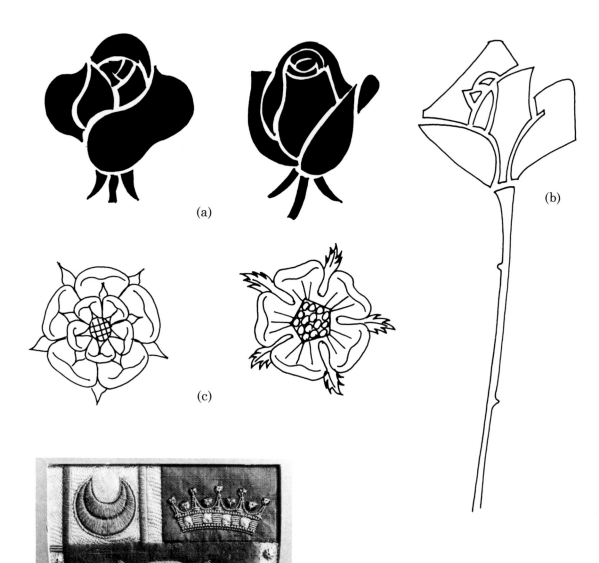

(a)

(b)

(c)

21 *Stylized roses.*
(a) Two Japanese symbols, showing the use of voiding – the narrow space between shapes which acts as a drawing line. This is often used in embroidery between areas of stitchery.
(b) The rose used by Lancôme make-up, presumably to symbolize dewy freshness.
(c) Two drawn heraldic roses, and an embroidered one using gold purl. The heraldic rose always has five petals, seeds in the centre of the flower, and tips of sepals showing between the petals.
(d) The Tudor rose is the white rose of York superimposed on the red rose of Lancaster, drawn here to suggest designs for i wadded quilting and ii appliqué or stuffed quilting.

(d) *i*

(d) *ii*

22 *A rubbing of another Javanese printing block, with a design of formal flowers and leaves flowing against a geometric background pattern. This contrast is very effective and can also be seen in gardens where flowers grow on walls, in window boxes, or against a trellis.*

23

23 *After the flowers come the seedheads, a wonder-ful collection of shapes. Try drawing the whole shape from the outside, and then cut it in half either horizontally or vertically to get a completely differ-ent pattern. The photograph and drawings show seedheads of:*
(a) & (b) poppies;
(c) aquilegia;
(d) honesty;
(e) & (f) Victorian engravings of seedheads;
(g) drawing of a cross-section of a banksia seedhead by Jan Messent.

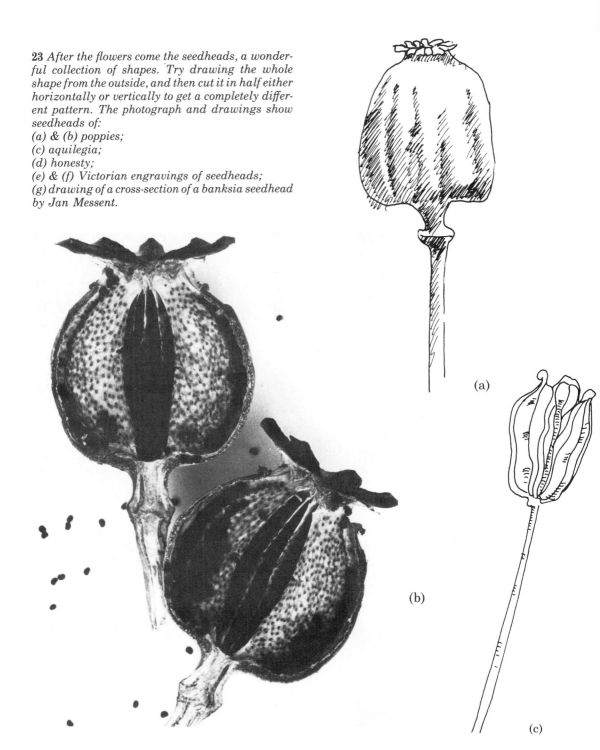

(a)

(b)

(c)

24

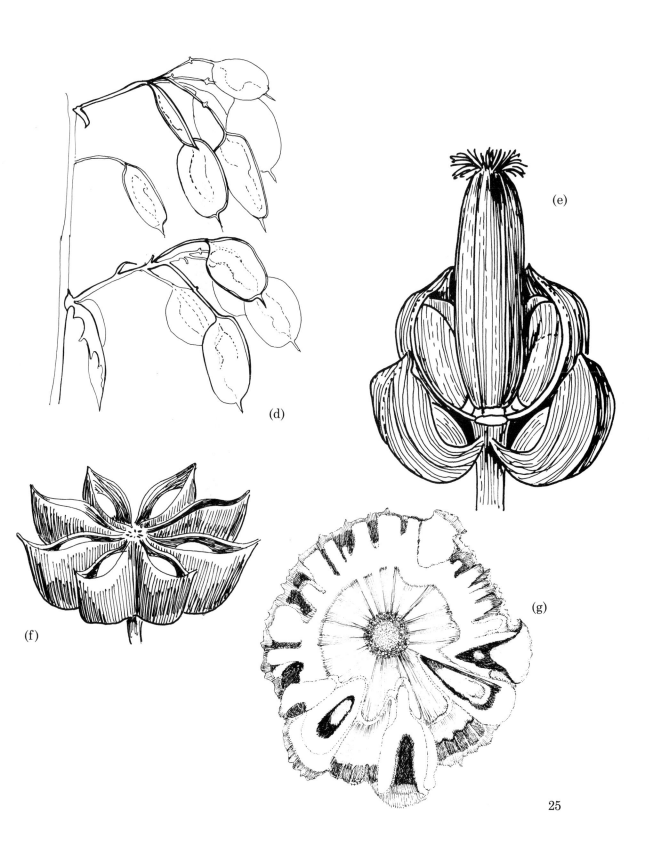

(d)

(e)

(f)

(g)

25

24 *Pen drawing of a collection of pine cones by Jan*
Messent, showing a great variety of detail.

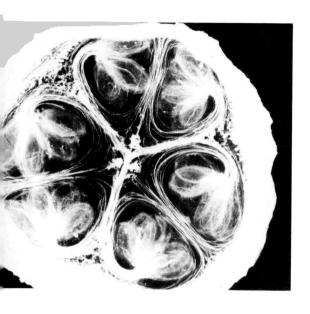

25 *Fruit and vegetables can also be a rich source of pattern. An extremely thin slice of a vegetable such as courgette or cucumber can be mounted between glass and projected on to a white wall to see more detail. If a piece of paper is taped to the wall and the slide projected on to the paper, then the pattern can be drawn.*

26 *An apple core, embroidered by Wendy Williams. The base is made of self-hardening clay covered with stretch fabric, with surface stitchery added to suggest bite marks. A seed has been included.*

27 *'The Golden Apple of the Hesperides', by Jennie Parry. This is a papier mâché apple covered with fabric and embroidery worked in gold threads. The lacy leaves are worked on a wire foundation.*

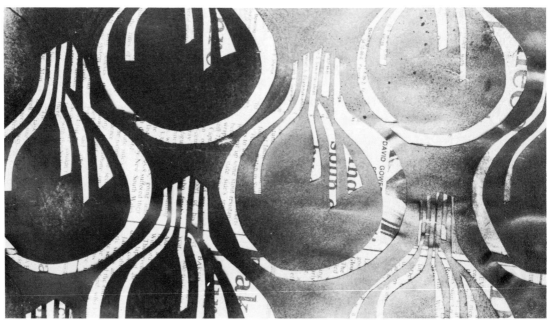

28 (Left) *Part of an investigation into onions, by Vivien Prideaux. First there is a photograph of a group of onions, and a slightly enlarged photocopy of it. Next to these, a piece of stiff plastic has been laid over some dried onion skins to give colour, and the pattern drawn on the plastic with a black felt pen.*

29 (Left, below) *A cut paper design of onions, sprayed with car spray paint, glued to newspaper.*

30 (Right) *Stuffed and corded quilting.*

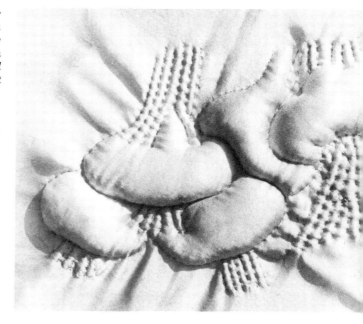

31 *Onion jacket, by Vivien Prideaux.*

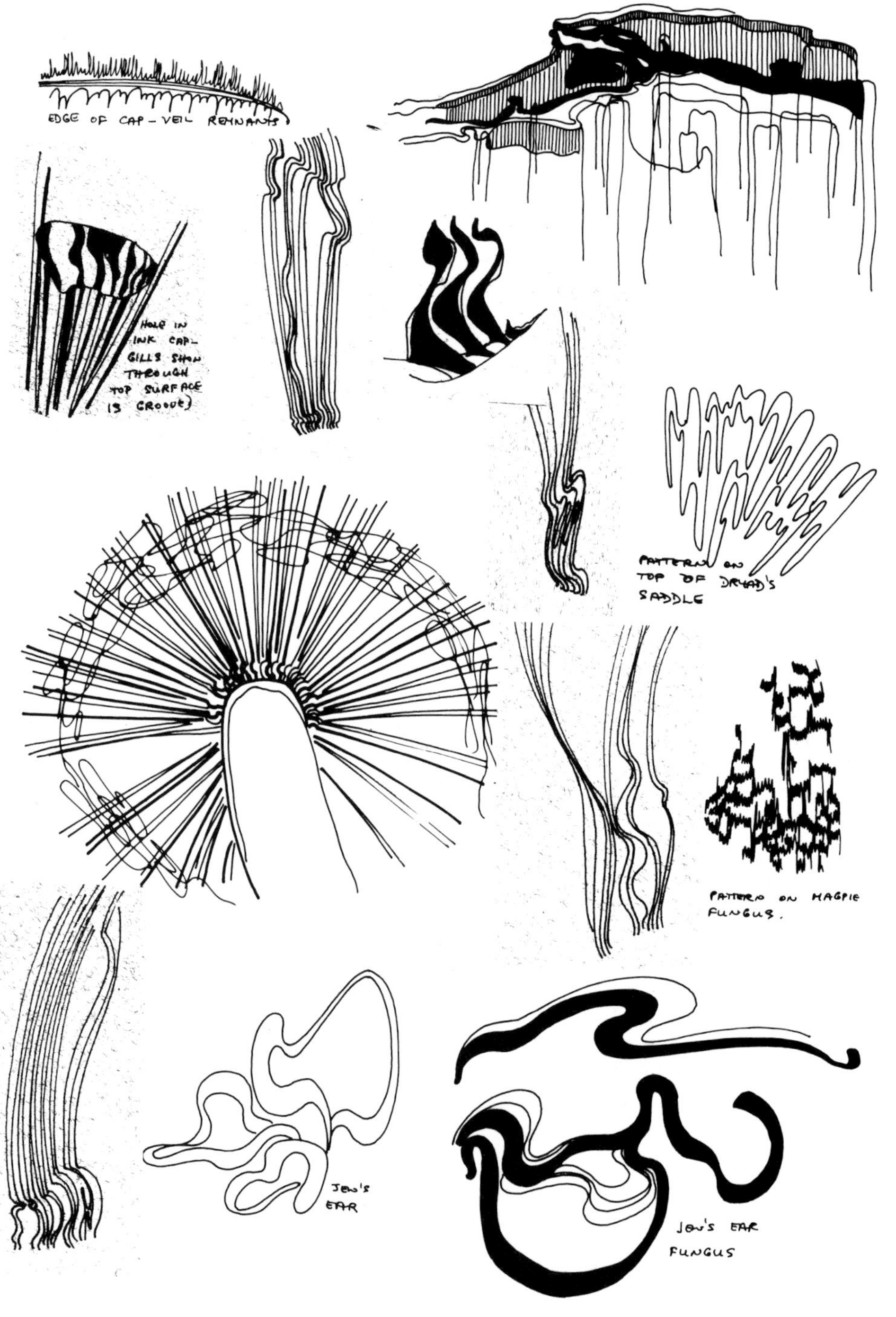
EDGE OF CAP - VEIL REMNANTS
HOLE IN INK CAP- GILLS SHOW THROUGH TOP SURFACE IS GROOVED)
PATTERN ON TOP OF DRYAD'S SADDLE
PATTERN ON MAGPIE FUNGUS.
JEW'S EAR
JEW'S EAR FUNGUS

32 *A page from my sketchbook, with patterns from mushrooms and other fungi.*

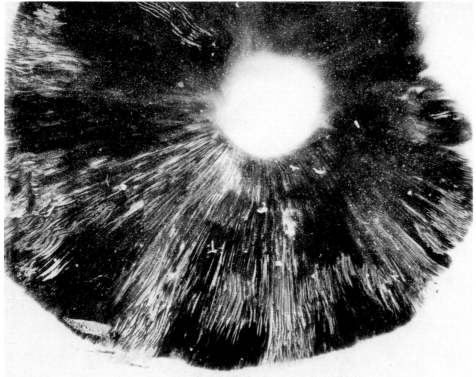

33 (Top) *The gill pattern of a horse mushroom found in a churchyard.*

34 *Spore print made by laying a fresh mushroom on a clean piece of paper, and leaving it overnight.*

35 *Field mushrooms, showing the gill patterns.*

36 (Below) *Embroidery based on fig. 35, worked on water-soluble fabric using machine embroidery. The fabric was tightly framed, the embroidery worked using variegated metal thread, and then the fabric dissolved in boiling water. The embroidery was pinned out on a cork bath mat to dry, and then applied to another piece of fabric. The whole work was then quilted through wadding.*

37 (Opposite) *A much-enlarged photocopy of fig. 35, which gives quite a different look, and suggests free smocking with beads or stitches. To enlarge a photograph as much as this, place it on a photocopier, enlarge it as much as the machine will allow, then place the photocopy on the machine and enlarge that. Continue to enlarge each successive photocopy until you get the result you want – often after six or more processes.*

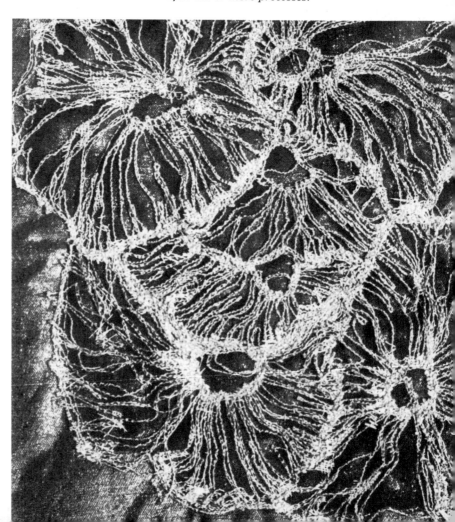

38 *The delicacy of lichen and its lace-like structure suggests fine needleweaving or machine-made lace.*

39 *In contrast, the thick leathery solidity of this Jew's-ear fungus suggests fabric manipulation, using fabric which has previously been embroidered.*

40 *This charcoal drawing of fungus growing on a tree has much less solidity and could be interpreted in transparent fabrics, with fine stitchery giving smooth blending of the tones or colours.*

41 *Get as close as you can when taking photographs and you will discover detail in unexpected places, as in this view of a cornfield. The different directions of* the ears of barley suggest stitchery in layers to give the same feeling of movement.

PHOTOGRAMS

To make photograms without a darkroom you will need: photographic paper, developing solution, fixer, three flat dishes large enough to take the paper, and a 100-watt clear bulb suspended about five feet above a table. You should work in the kitchen with the curtains drawn, but the room does not need to be absolutely blacked out. Leave just enough light to see your way around after your eyes have got used to the dark. Dilute the developer and fixer according to the instructions on the bottle – you will need about 1½–2 pints of each solution. Pour them into two of the dishes. Half fill the third dish with clean water. All the solutions should be at room temperature (about 68°F). Turn all lights off,

place a piece of photographic paper under the 100-watt bulb, and arrange your grasses, leaves etc., on it. Switch the light on for about 60 seconds. Turn the light off. Place the paper in the developer in the dish, and leave it for about one minute until the background has gone black, rocking it gently part of the time. Rinse the paper in the clean water, and slide it into the fixer. Leave it for about five minutes, rocking it every so often. Then wash the photogram under running water for 30 minutes. The times are variable, and if the first one is too dark, shorten the exposure time. If too pale, lengthen it. Leave the photogram to dry, hanging by the corner from a clothes peg.

42 *A photogram of grasses.*

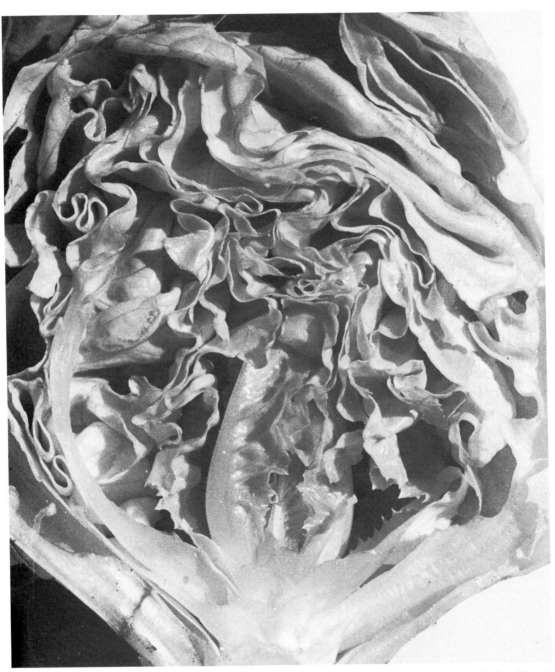

43 Cross-section of a lettuce which suggests the use of ruched or gathered fabric between padded areas. The edges of the fabric could be embroidered, bleached, or burnt. To burn fabric, hold it in a candle flame until it just starts to catch fire. Blow it out instantly, and burn the next bit. Rub the dark edges to get rid of any loose pieces of burnt fabric.

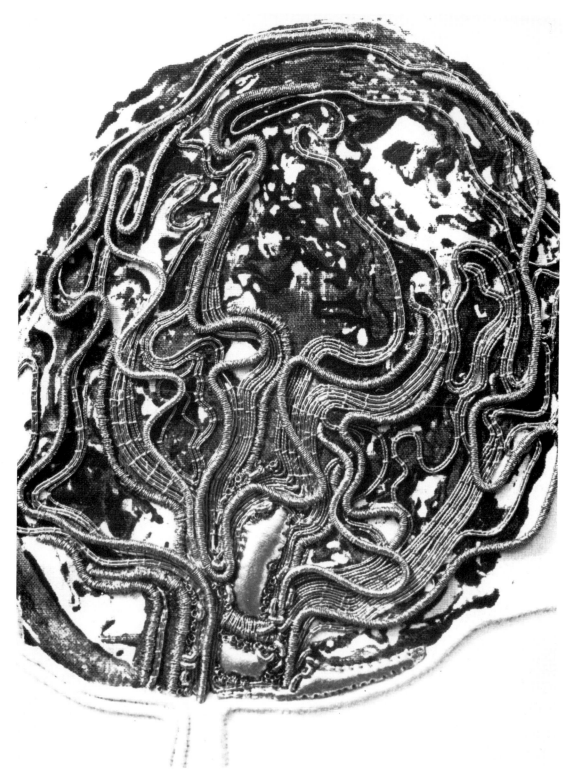

44 *A cabbage, printed on to fabric by painting the cut side with fabric paint, and then pressing it on to a piece of silk. The fabric is then ironed to fix the paint. The embroidery is worked in gold threads couched flat, small areas of padded kid, and string wrapped with fine gold thread couched over the top.*

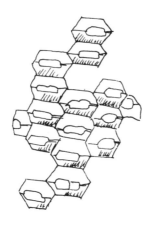

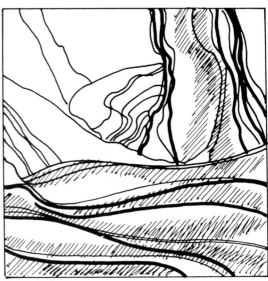

45 *Drawings of an ear of corn in pen, ink and wash, and pencil. The details of the kernels suggest tiny padded pieces with holes in them, showing another colour through.*

46 *Drawing by Jan Messent of an ear of corn.*

47 *(Above right) An investigation into the qualities of corn, using paper made thoroughly wet by drawing it through a dish of mixed Polycell. The paper was torn, folded, pleated, scrumpled and twisted to get the feeling of movement and the textures observed in the corn. When dry, the results are fairly stiff and durable.*

48 *The same feeling of movement translated into felt, using the cut-through method of appliqué. Two (or three) layers of felt of different colours are placed together, and a tracing of a design placed on top. Pin through all three layers. The lines of the design are machine stitched and the paper torn away. The top layer of felt is then cut away in parts to show the under colour.*

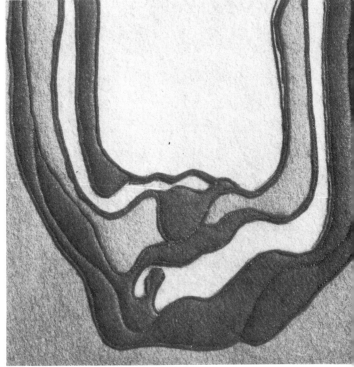

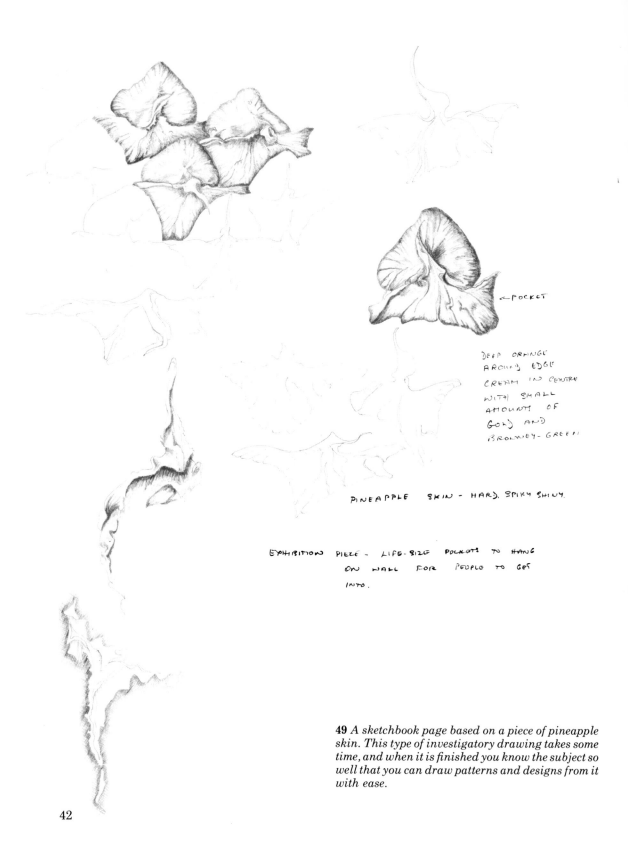

←POCKET

DEEP ORANGE
AROUND EDGE
CREAM IN CENTRE
WITH SMALL
AMOUNTS OF
GOLD AND
BROWNEY-GREEN

PINEAPPLE SKIN - HARD, SPIKY, SHINY.

EXHIBITION PIECE - LIFE-SIZE POCKETS TO HANG
ON WALL FOR PEOPLE TO GET
INTO.

49 *A sketchbook page based on a piece of pineapple skin. This type of investigatory drawing takes some time, and when it is finished you know the subject so well that you can draw patterns and designs from it with ease.*

50 *Repeat patterns based on the pineapple skin drawings. These could be worked in free stitchery, inlay or appliqué, quilting, or the grid version in patchwork.*

43

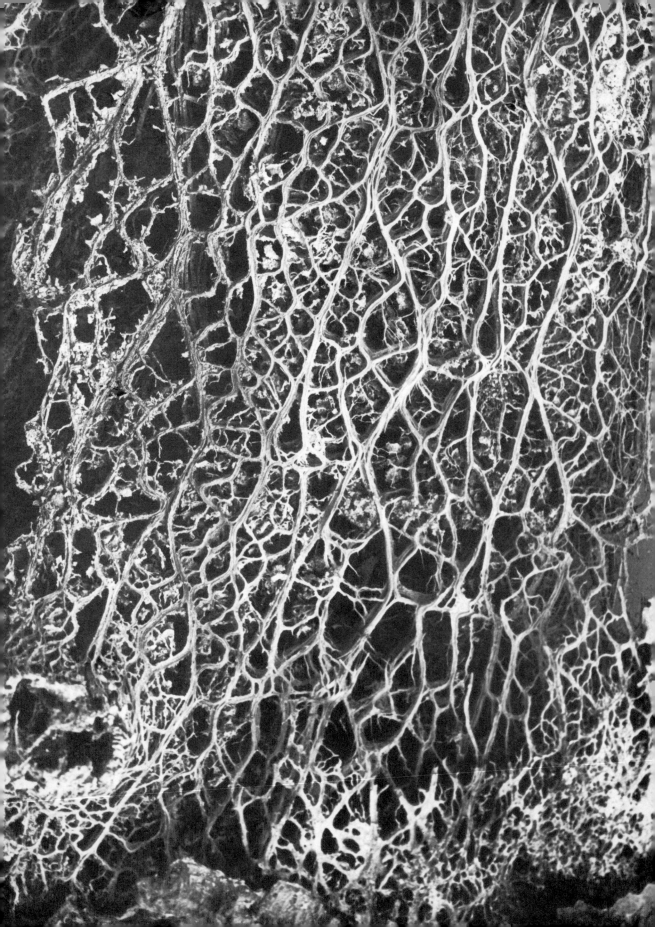

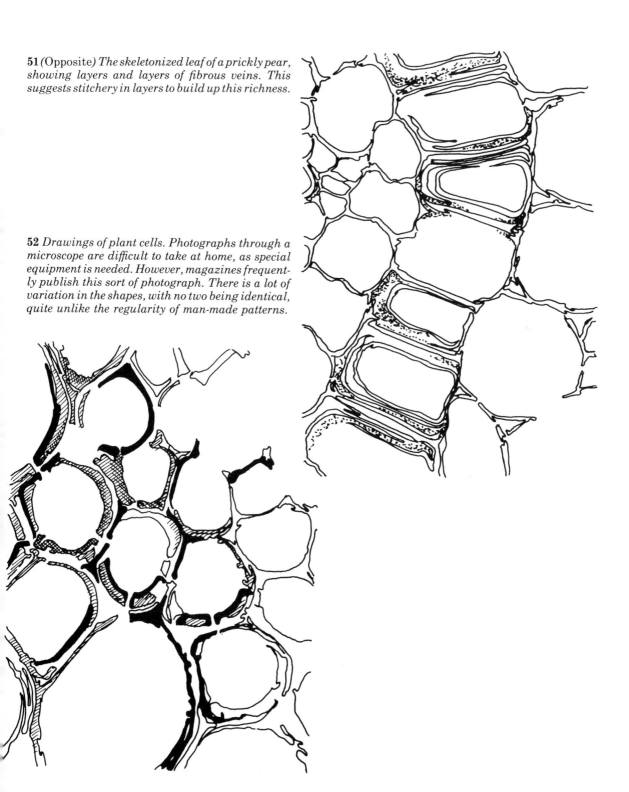

51 (Opposite) *The skeletonized leaf of a prickly pear, showing layers and layers of fibrous veins. This suggests stitchery in layers to build up this richness.*

52 *Drawings of plant cells. Photographs through a microscope are difficult to take at home, as special equipment is needed. However, magazines frequently publish this sort of photograph. There is a lot of variation in the shapes, with no two being identical, quite unlike the regularity of man-made patterns.*

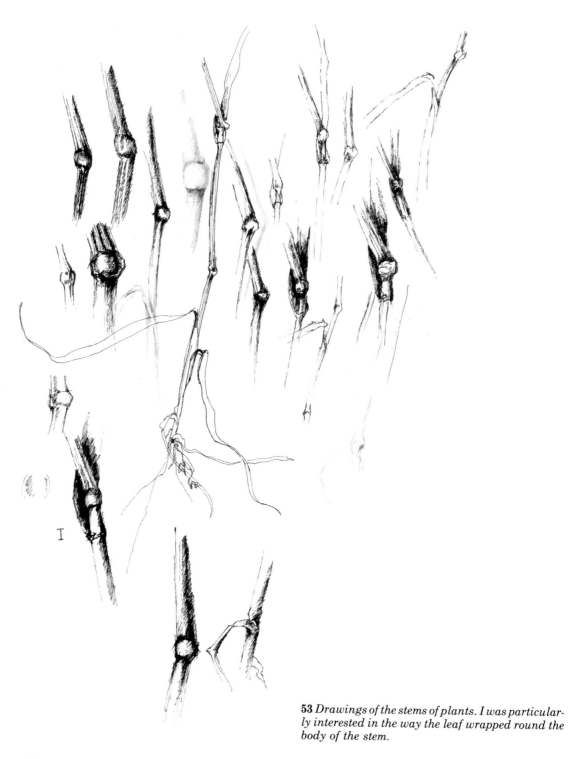

53 Drawings of the stems of plants. I was particularly interested in the way the leaf wrapped round the body of the stem.

54 *A piece of ivy root, bleached by the weather.*

55 *Drawing by Val du Cros of details of sections of a corn cob in fine pen and pencil. Investigation like this into detail results in plenty of ideas for irregular pattern, with interest in the variations of the small shapes.*

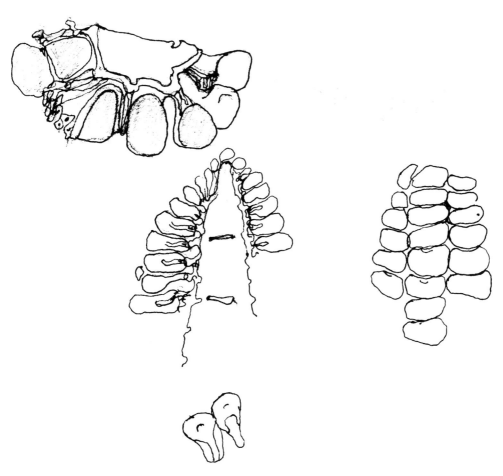

56 *Withered and wrinkled skin has a very papery feel, and sometimes shreds into separate fibres, which suggests shredded and wrinkled metallic fabric. By isolating areas of the photograph, different designs can be seen to emerge.*

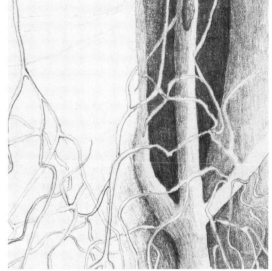

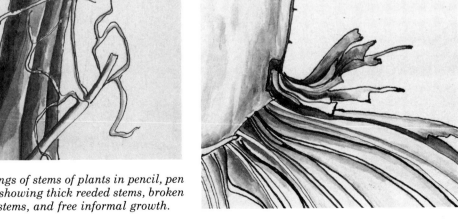

57 *More drawings of stems of plants in pencil, pen and ink wash, showing thick reeded stems, broken and shredded stems, and free informal growth.*

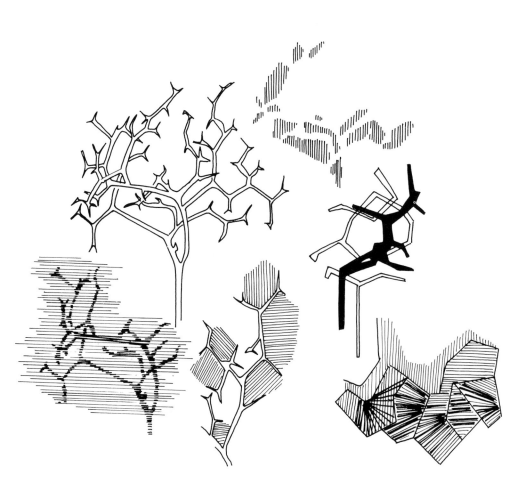

58 *A stylized drawing of a thorn bush, with some suggestions for patterns using sections of the drawing. Lines in a drawing suggest lines of stitchery.*

TWO

DESIGN USING PATTERN FROM NATURE

Pattern means, to embroiderers, a decorative design on a surface: usually of stitchery on fabric. A pattern must have repetition. This is usually of a shape, but it can also be the repetition of the spaces between shapes, of an area of texture, or of a colour. Regular patterns are easier to understand than haphazard ones, and patterns designed by man are usually regular. Patterns found in nature are usually more complicated than man-made ones, with more variation in the individual units. The shapes are similar and echo each other, and we often find this more interesting than exact repeats.

The size of the unit in a pattern can vary slightly, and so can the colour. In fact, changing the colour is a very good way of making a regular pattern more interesting, while the exact repetition of the shape gives a structure which holds the design together.

This chapter suggests many ways of designing using pattern.

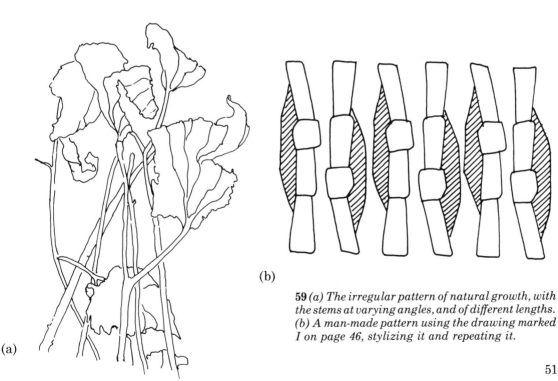

(a)

(b)

59 *(a) The irregular pattern of natural growth, with the stems at varying angles, and of different lengths. (b) A man-made pattern using the drawing marked I on page 46, stylizing it and repeating it.*

THE PRINCIPLES OF PATTERN

There is a language associated with pattern, which describes certain arrangements of a motif. In addition to the ones on this page, motifs can be arranged in straight or curved lines to make border patterns, and this will be shown later on in the book.

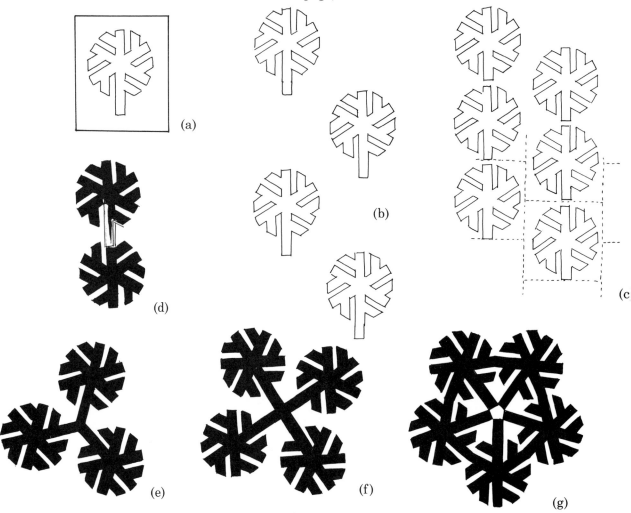

(a)

(b)

(c

(d)

(e)

(f)

(g)

60 *(a) The motif, which is a tree from a Japanese trade mark.*
(b) The tree used in a spot pattern.
(c) The tree as a half-drop repeat. This can be either horizontal or vertical, when it is called a brick pattern.
(d), (e), (f) & (g) Arrangements using two, three, four and five motifs. These can be used as spot patterns or half-drop repeats.

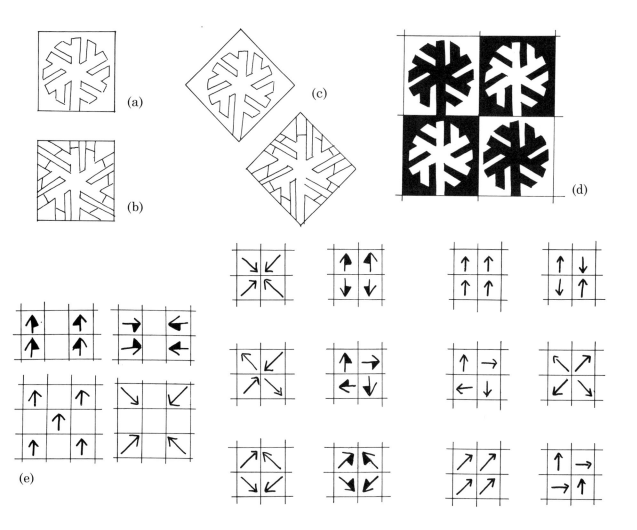

61 *When the motif or a pattern is placed inside a square, diamond or any other shape that will repeat, it is called a block.*

(a) shows the tree in a square block;

(b) the same tree with the straight lines continued to the edges of the block to make a slightly different design;

(c) the same trees inside diamond-shaped blocks;

(d) the most usual repeat, with four blocks placed together all facing the same way. When alternate backgrounds and motifs are filled in as here, it makes a counterchange pattern.

(e) Some of the ways that a block can be arranged to make different patterns. With an asymmetrical block, the differences can be amazing.

(f) Two patterns, showing how different the same block can look.

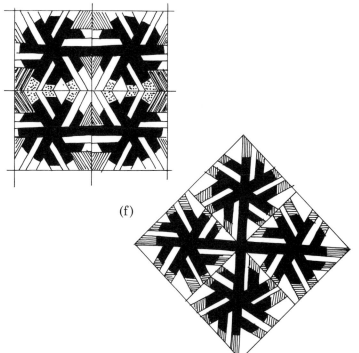

(a)

(b)

(c)

(d)

(e)

(f)

(g)

62 *(a) A tracing from an advertisement, with the dotted lines outlining areas of different colours. (b), (c), (d), (e) & (f) Parts of the motif arranged in pairs face to face, back to back, or end to end, to make new patterns.*

54

63 *Parts of the same flower motif arranged in groups of three, four and five to make symmetrical designs. This sort of linear design is particularly suitable for wadded quilting, appliqué or cut work, and could be used on clothes or household articles.*

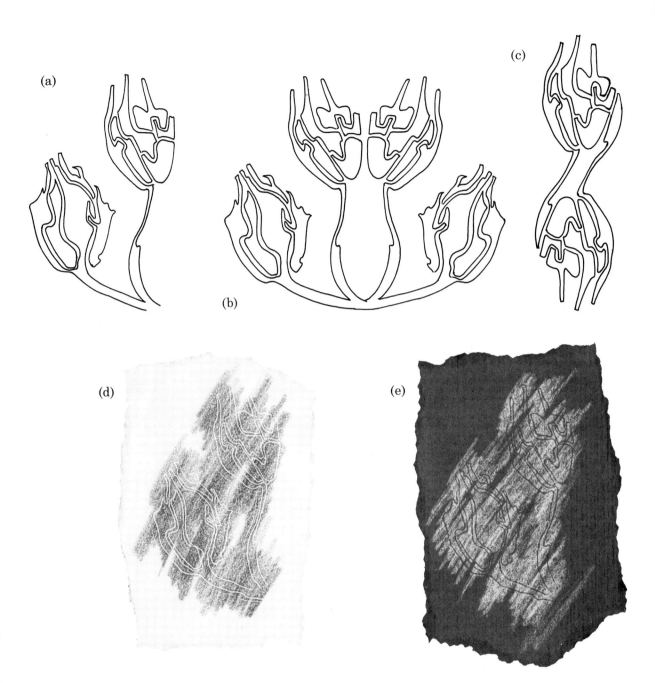

64 *(a) Line drawing of a seedhead.*
(b) Arranged to make a semi-circular pattern. One motif is a mirror-image of the other.
(c) Part of the motif arranged end to end.
(d) & (e) Indented drawings. Trace a motif and lay the tracing on top of a piece of cartridge paper. Place a folded newspaper underneath as padding. Draw over the lines of the tracing, using a ballpoint pen
and pressing hard to impress lines on the cartridge paper. Remove the tracing and gently rub over the surface of the cartridge paper with a wax crayon, coloured pencil or chalk. You can use streaks of different colours to make the result more interesting, and the paper can be white, black, or coloured. This design can be translated into stitchery which is then quilted or overstitched to define the motif.

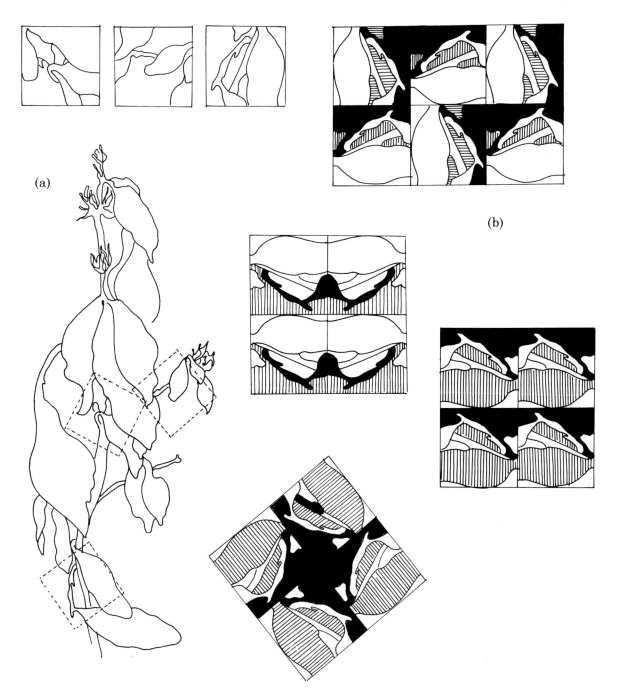

(a)

(b)

BLOCK DESIGNS FROM A DRAWING

65 *(a) 4-cm (1½-inch) squares are drawn on tracing paper and placed over different parts of a drawing or design, trying different angles to find interesting patterns. Trace what you see inside the square.*
(b) Choose one and trace it as a repeat pattern with six, eight or nine blocks together. The blocks can all face the same way, or different ways. Colour in each block the same, using three or four colours. Then you can trace the pattern again and try different colourways.*

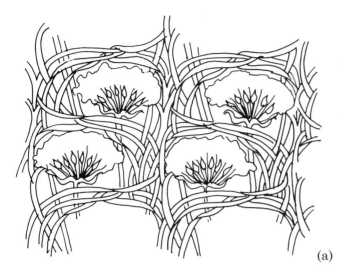

66 *(a) A pattern drawn from a piece of wrapping paper.*
(b) Part of the pattern enclosed in a rectangular block and repeated.
(c) The design was enlarged on the photocopier and part of it enclosed in a rectangular block.

(a)

(b)

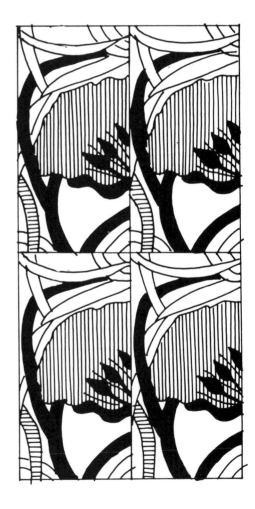

(c)

58

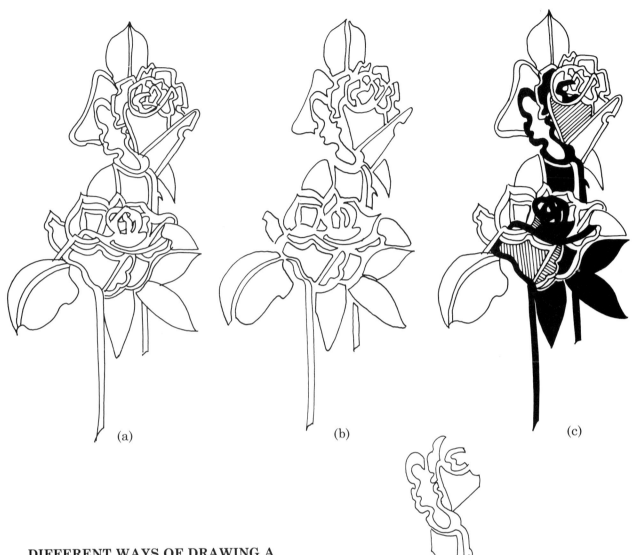

(a)   (b)   (c)

(d)

DIFFERENT WAYS OF DRAWING A MOTIF TO SUGGEST DIFFERENT TYPES OF EMBROIDERY

67 *(a) Drawing of two roses. The originals were on a greetings card, but have been arranged to make a new design.*

(b) A way of drawing to suggest stuffed quilting, appliqué or separate areas of stitchery. This is another example of voiding.

(c) Tone is added to give a focal point to the design. The darkest tone could be either the strongest colour or the areas of solid stitchery, in contrast to stitchery outlining the other shapes.

(d) These areas have been isolated to make a new design with different qualities.

59

THE USE OF LINE

Line can define a shape, or be used as a filling. When drawing or designing, try to use different thicknesses of line to give an illusion of depth. A thicker line will come forward and a thinner one recede, as shown in these illustrations. The line can be drawn with a pen or pencil, a brush, be an engraved line as in a printing block, or be a stitched line. It can change along its length and become thinner or thicker. It can be straight, curved, broken or dotted, long or short, jagged or wiggly. There is such an enormous variety of embroidery stitches and threads that all these lines can easily be translated into them. Although there are no lines, as such, in nature, it is a convention that we use when drawing or designing to indicate an edge of a shape or area, and it is so often used that is worth looking at the different qualities of line that it is possible to make.

68 (a) *This design looks flat because the lines are all the same width.*
(b) *This one has depth because thick and thin lines are used.*

(a)

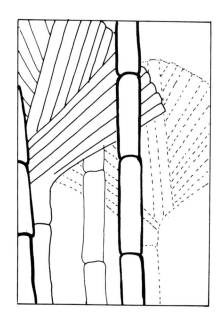

(b)

(a)

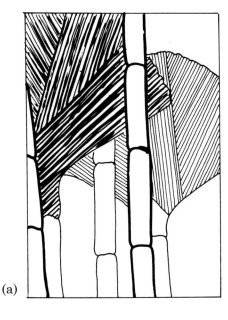

(a)

(b)

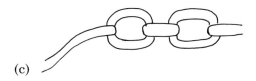

(c)

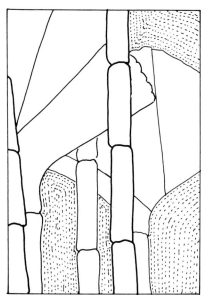

(b)

(d)

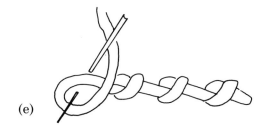

(e)

69 (Above) *Line used as fillings.*
(a) Lines in different directions in different areas of the design suggest lines of stitching.
(b) A combination of solid and broken lines suggests stitchery or the edges of pieces of fabric, with the broken lines used as a background filling.

70 *Some line stitches which could be used to embroider these designs.*
(a) Running stitch.
(b) Whipped back stitch.
(c) Cable chain stitch.
(d) Twisted chain stitch.
(e) Coral stitch.

61

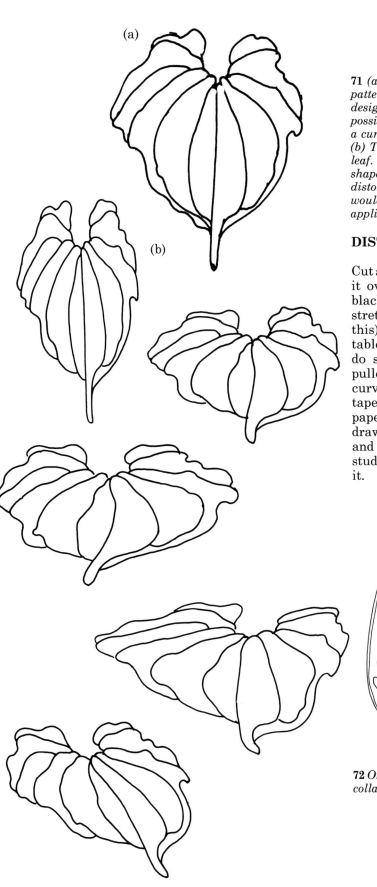

(a)

(b)

71 *(a) A leaf with an interesting shape and vein patterns. This leaf can be used as it is in any of the design methods previously described, but it is also possible to alter or distort the shape, perhaps to fit in a curve.*
(b) These are some of the results of distorting the leaf. As we are so used to seeing many different shapes of leaves, and curled and withered leaves, the distorted shapes do not strike us as peculiar. It would be a different matter if the same process was applied to the human figure.

DISTORTING A MOTIF

Cut a piece of old stocking or tights, and place it over a drawing. Trace the motif with a black felt pen on to the stocking (do not stretch the stocking while you are doing this). Then tape the stocking drawing on to a table or board, pulling it out of shape as you do so. It can be lengthened, made wider, pulled from opposite corners, or even in a curve. Pull the stocking really hard as you tape it. Then place a new piece of tracing paper over the top and trace the distorted drawing. This process is very quick and easy and was passed on to me by one of my students, so I cannot claim to have invented it.

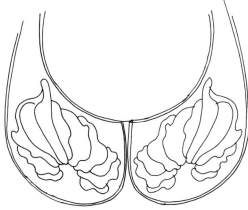

72 *One of the distorted shapes used in a design for a collar.*

73 *The same leaf used, overlapping, to make a pattern. It looks rather confused because of the lack of tone or colour.*

74 *The addition of tone in some areas, and the use of thick, thin and broken lines restore order to the pattern. Colour would help even more.*

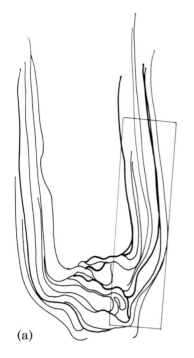

DESIGNS USING BLOCKS OF DIFFERENT SHAPES

75 *(a) A rectangular window is laid over a drawing, and a tracing made of what is inside the window. (b) The block.*

(a)

(b)

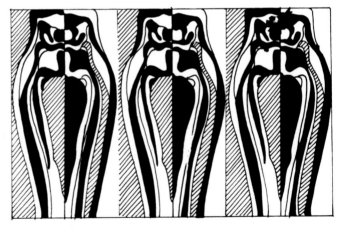

76 *Six blocks, three of them reversed to make mirror images, arranged in a line. Three tones have been used to make a counterchange pattern. This sort of design is particularly suitable for appliqué or inlay.*

(b)

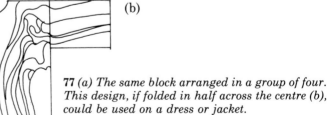

77 *(a) The same block arranged in a group of four. This design, if folded in half across the centre (b), could be used on a dress or jacket.*

(a)

78 *(a) Part of the same drawing within a lozenge-shaped block.*
(b) & (c) Four of these blocks arranged in groups of four.
(d) Three blocks arranged to make a hexagon. This shape can be repeated to make an all-over pattern.
(e) Another group of four blocks. The lines have been joined to cross the empty spaces.

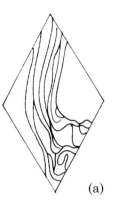

(a)

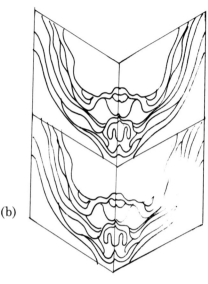

(b)

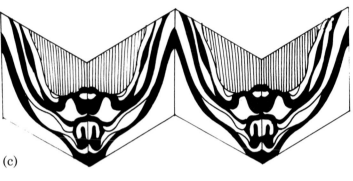

(c)

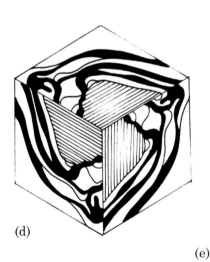

(d)

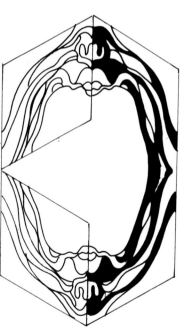

(e)

79 *(Far right) This design for a bag uses six of the blocks and could be carried out in appliqué and machine embroidery. I had thought of working it in creams, greys and black, in silks and satin, with a tassel at the point.*

65

80 *Carved plaster showing an Arabic pattern which uses formal leaf patterns in bands, together with bands of lettering.*

THREE

BORDERS & BANDS

Repeating a flower or leaf motif, design or block in a straight or curved line to make border patterns is nearly always successful because the repetition strengthens the design. Block patterns using flower designs in squares or triangles, single or double motifs, and parts of all-over patterns can all be repeated to make a border which can be fairly stylized or free and flowing. Borders can be used on clothes, lampshades, cushions, edges of curtains or pelmets, gussets of bags, or on quilts. Many borders or bands can be put together to make an all-over pattern of great richness.

The designs in this chapter show how you can put together some patterns to make borders, and you can do the same thing with your own drawings or tracings.

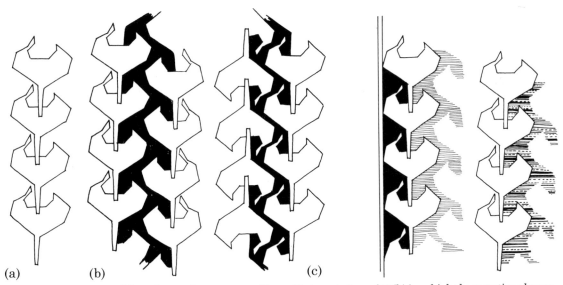

(a)   (b)   (c)

81 (Above) (a) *A motif based on onions arranged in an overlapping line, by Vivien Prideaux.*
(b) & (c) *Two of these lines put together facing the same way, and reversed. The negative shapes become nearly as interesting as the original design.*

82 *A variation of 81(b) in which the negative shapes are emphasized and the second line only suggested.*

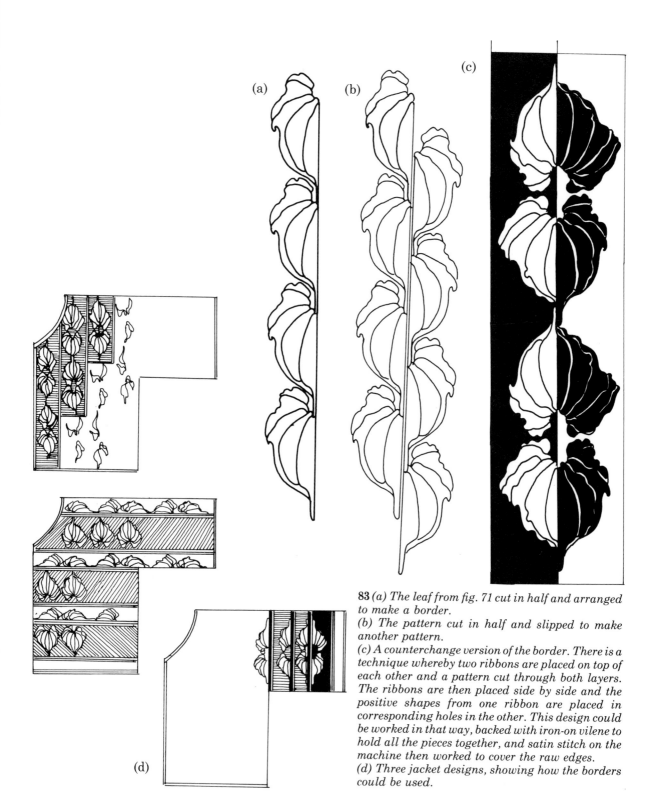

83 (a) The leaf from fig. 71 cut in half and arranged
to make a border.
(b) The pattern cut in half and slipped to make
another pattern.
(c) A counterchange version of the border. There is a
technique whereby two ribbons are placed on top of
each other and a pattern cut through both layers.
The ribbons are then placed side by side and the
positive shapes from one ribbon are placed in
corresponding holes in the other. This design could
be worked in that way, backed with iron-on vilene to
hold all the pieces together, and satin stitch on the
machine then worked to cover the raw edges.
(d) Three jacket designs, showing how the borders
could be used.

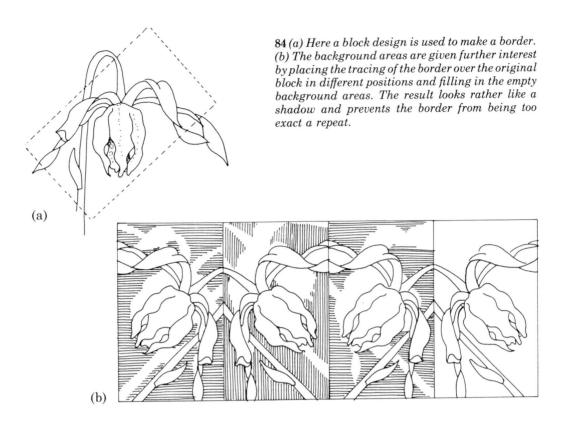

(a)

84 *(a) Here a block design is used to make a border. (b) The background areas are given further interest by placing the tracing of the border over the original block in different positions and filling in the empty background areas. The result looks rather like a shadow and prevents the border from being too exact a repeat.*

(b)

85 *(a) A semi-circular window can also be repeated to make a border, either as in (b), as a mirror image, or as in (c), separated by space.*

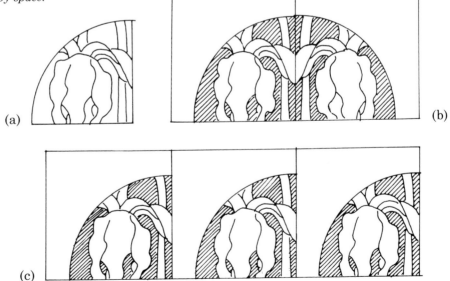

(a)

(b)

(c)

(a)

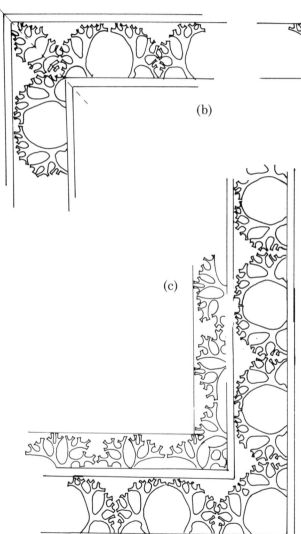

(b)

(c)

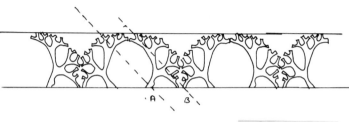

(d)

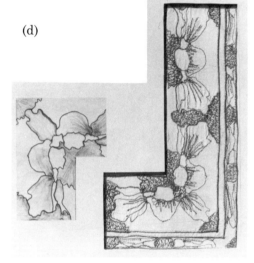

86 *(a) A branch of this tree is repeated to make wide and narrow border patterns.*
(b) To make a border turn a corner, draw a line across it at 45° using a protractor. Then trace the border up to the line, flip the tracing over, laying the first drawing at right angles to the line, and continue tracing. This corner design was made by drawing up to line B.
(c) A different corner made by tracing up to line A.
(d) An embroidered border by Bridget Dixon using machine embroidery in pinks and creams, with the pencil drawing of the original corner design.

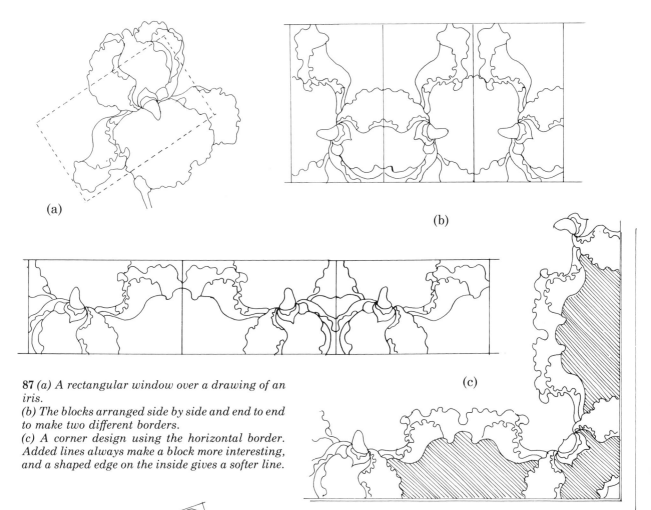

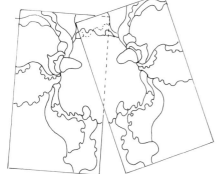

87 *(a) A rectangular window over a drawing of an iris.*
(b) The blocks arranged side by side and end to end to make two different borders.
(c) A corner design using the horizontal border. Added lines always make a block more interesting, and a shaped edge on the inside gives a softer line.

88 *(a) To make curved patterns from blocks, overlap the blocks at the inner curves and extend the lines over the spaces at the bottom.*
(b) A design for a curved neckline or mirror frame. This could be worked in appliqué and machine embroidery, or in two layers of transparent fabrics with parts cut away and machine embroidery added.

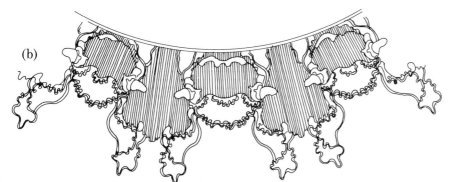

71

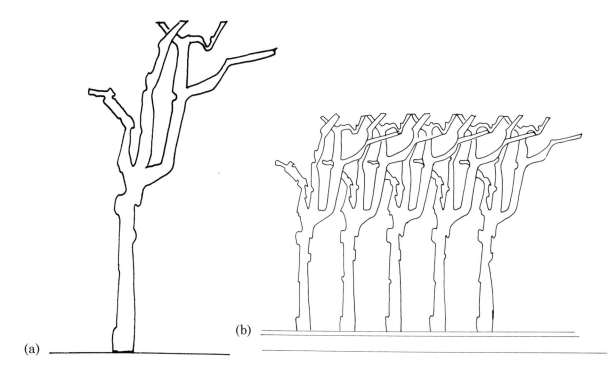

(a)

(b)

(c)

89 (a) A border built up by repeating a single motif, in this case a winter tree.
(b) The overlapped shapes making a border.
(c) Some areas filled in with tone to suggest areas of different colours or textures.
(d) Tracing (b) was placed over tracing (c), moved slightly so that is was not directly on top of it, and some of the dark areas filled in. Extra lines were added to the trees to suggest lines of stitchery.

72

(d)

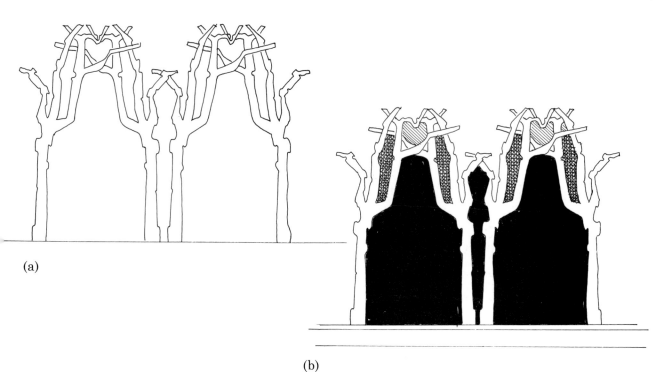

(a)

(b)

90 *(a) The same trees, with alternate ones reversed to make another border.*
(b) Areas of tone giving quite a different effect from 89 (c).
(c) A design for a cushion. It could be carried out in needleweaving over a fabric ground, and worked in layers to give the effect of entwined spiky branches. When the design is enlarged (in this case to cushion size) obviously the spaces in the tree trunks and branches will be larger, so more than one band of needleweaving will be needed to fill the areas. This gives the opportunity for more colours and thread textures to be included.

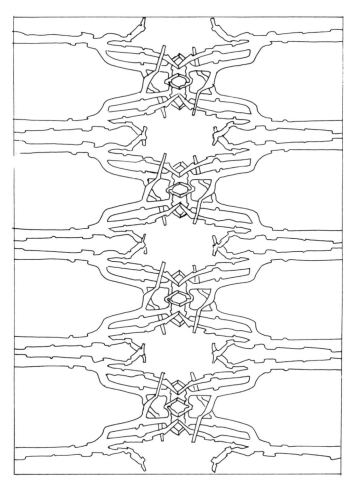

(c)

(a)

(b)

91 *(a) & (b) Two border patterns designed by Bridget Dixon. She made a printing block by gluing string to a piece of card in the shape of a rose. The background pattern was made by rolling an ink-covered rubber roller over the paper using gold ink, and black roses were printed on top. This is a quick way of designing and makes it easy to do many versions to judge the layout and proportions of a design.*

74

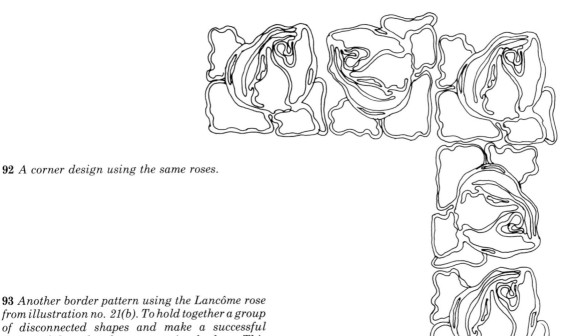

92 *A corner design using the same roses.*

93 *Another border pattern using the Lancôme rose from illustration no. 21(b). To hold together a group of disconnected shapes and make a successful design of them, lay them on a strip of colour. This can be a length of ribbon, stitchery, or a stripe already on a printed or woven fabric.*

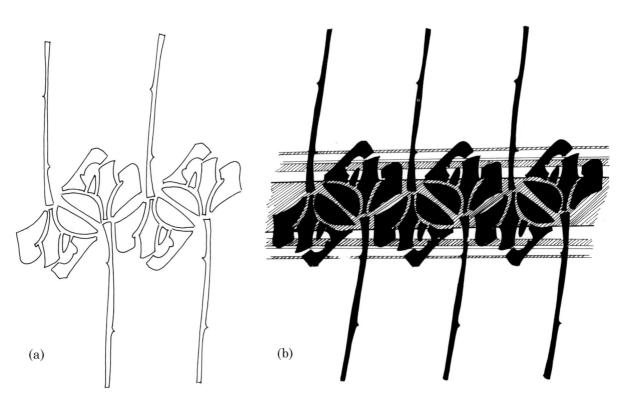

(a)

(b)

FOUR

SILHOUETTES FROM FLOWERS & PLANTS

A silhouette usually shows only the outline of an object, as in this drawing of a group of mushrooms with the silhouette next to it. However, I will include a little detail in some cases, such as the veins of the leaves, to add interest. A silhouette is interesting only if the shape is an interesting one, with enough detail to catch your attention. It can be dark against a light background, or light against a dark one. The background need not be plain, and can be patterned, textured or multi-coloured. In embroidery the background has often been embroidered, leaving the silhouette in plain fabric. This is a great help, as it is often difficult to decide exactly how to embroider a flower or leaf design, whereas it is much easier to think of ways of treating the background.

This chapter suggests different ways of designing backgrounds for silhouettes leading to embroidery.

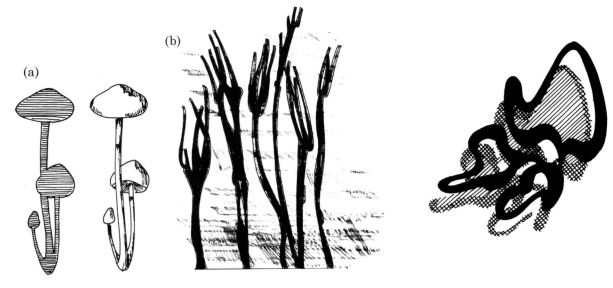

94 (a) Drawing of mushrooms with the silhouette. (b) Silhouette of lichen against a background of a rubbing of pencils in a box. The straight lines and areas of texture contrast with the flowing lines of the lichen.

95 Pattern from fig. 32 used against its own shadow. This could be stitchery against a printed shape or heavy stitchery against areas of running stitch or darning.

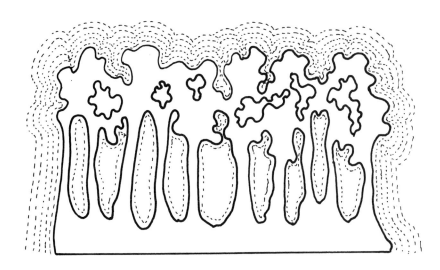

96 *Contour lines around the silhouette of a group of trees suggest quilting around appliqué.*

97 *A drawing by Jan Messent of horse chestnut leaves, with a textured background which suggests massed stitchery – perhaps Cretan stitch or blanket stitch in layers.*

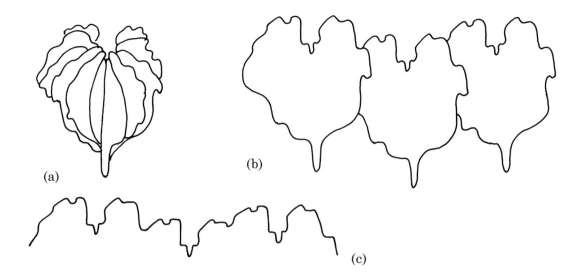

(a)

(b)

(c)

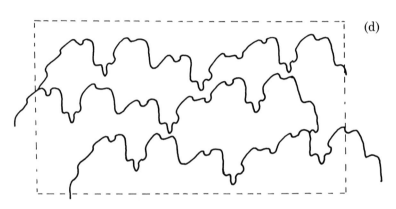

(d)

(e)

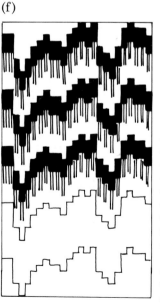

(f)

98 *Building up an all-over pattern using a single shape.*
(a) A leaf.
(b) Drawing around the shape three times to make an overlapping pattern.
(c) Tracing of the top line of the pattern.
(d) Tracing (c) repeated three times, shifted slightly each time to add interest.
(e) The pattern turned upside-down, with tone added to make it look like overlapping shapes. Stitchery would be heaviest where the darkest areas are.
(f) The same design drawn on squared paper, making a design for Florentine work on canvas.

99 *A panel by Jane Lemon using a drawing of a pot of geraniums. The silhouette is padded, and the background is a mass of machine embroidery in blues and greens. The frame is wrapped in the same blues and greens, but the tones are reversed.*

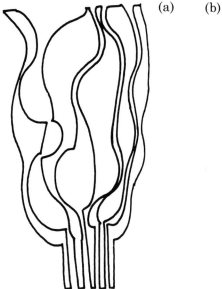

(a)   (b)

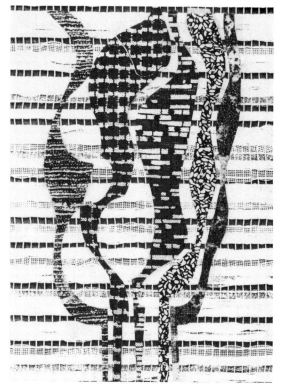

100 *More ways of designing backgrounds for silhouettes.*
(a) A stylized tree.
(b) The design was enlarged and a cut paper design made of it, using photocopies of fabrics. This is easy to do – just lay a piece of fabric on a photocopier and press the button. It can be carried out in appliqué using the same fabrics, perhaps with solid stitchery in some areas to give contrast.

101 (Left) *Another tree shape was cut from black paper and glued to a piece of paper which I had printed with a piece of card. To do this, paint the edge of a card strip with paint, or fabric paint if working straight on to the fabric, and press it on to the paper. Build up the texture in different colours to represent stitchery.*

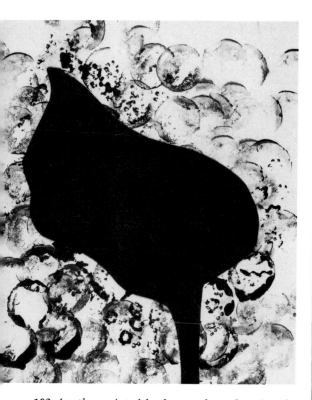

102 *Another printed background, made using the end of a dowel rod and a drinking straw.*

103 *Drawing by Julia Barton of flowers in white chalk against a background of painted texture in many colours.*

(a)

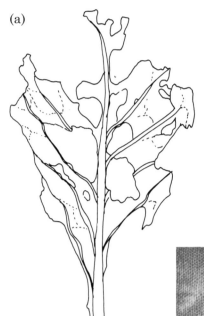

104 *(a) A drawing of a cabbage leaf partly eaten by slugs. A wonderful shape such as this is very inspiring.*

(b) The same leaf in white organdie applied to black net, laid over a background of burnt strips of organza in pinks, blues, lilac and grey. The edges of the net were also burnt. All the layers are held together with tiny stitches.

(c) Machine-made lace leaf applied to fabric. The leaf was worked in variegated thread in straight stitch and satin stitch on hot-water soluble fabric which was then dissolved. It was laid on to space dyed fabric in similar colours to the stitching, placed over layers of wadding and backing, and then quilted.

(c)

(b)

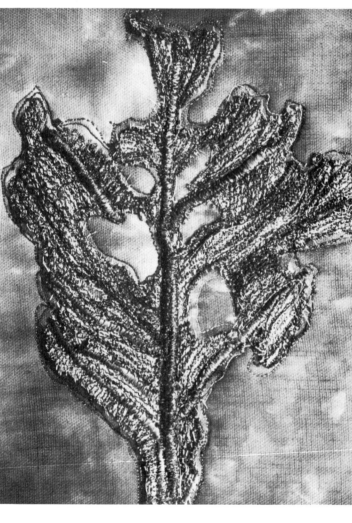

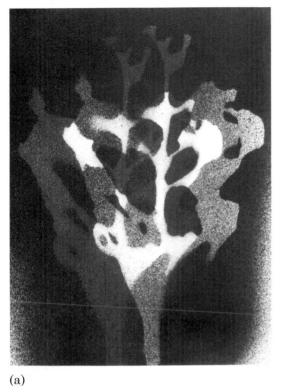

(a)

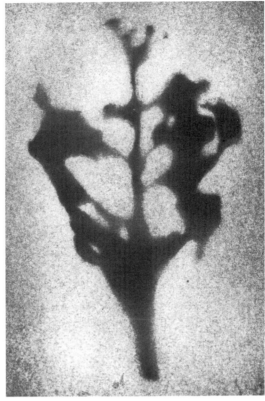

(b)

(c)

105 *(a) The cabbage leaf was laid on black paper and sprayed with black car spray paint. It was then moved and sprayed again to give this shadow image.*
(b) The leaf was laid on black paper and sprayed with white car spray paint.
(c) The background of this design was embroidered in red and gold threads, using a machine zigzag stitch, on space dyed fabric. Small gold beads were added to give highlights.

83

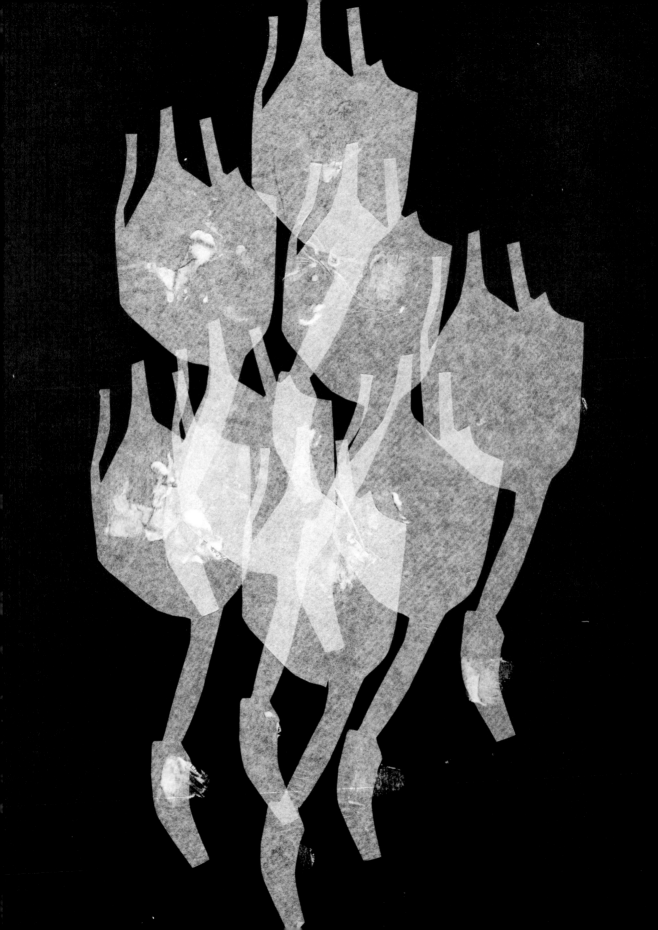

106 (Left) *One of the easiest ways to design using silhouettes is to cut the shape many times from white tissue paper and to arrange it on black paper to make an overlapping pattern. Make sure that the shapes formed by the doubled layers of tissue are not too complicated.*

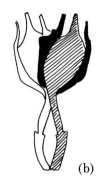

(a)

(b)

(c)

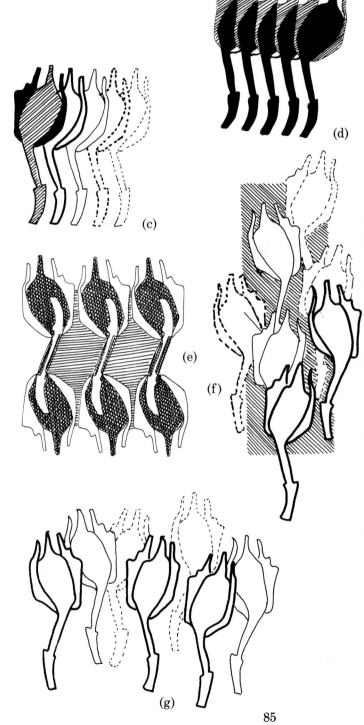

(d)

(e)

(f)

107 *Patterns using the overlapped shape of a seedhead.*
(a) The original seedhead.
(b), (c), (d) & (e) Simple patterns using the seedhead shape.
(f) & (g) More interesting designs, with thicker lines making a focal point or centre of interest.
These could be interpreted in quilting, or as printed shapes with line and solid stitchery.

Very often the use to which an embroidery is to be put will suggest the techniques or type of stitchery. If you want to make a lampshade, then shadow work, or fabric and threads trapped between layers of transparent fabric, would allow the light to shine through. If you want to make a cushion, then appliqué and machine embroidery would be the right choice.

(g)

To transfer a design on to graph paper to use for counted thread work, this is the procedure. Draw the design on white paper with a black pen. Tape it to a window pane, and tape a piece of graph paper over it. Trace the design on to the graph paper exactly as it is, using a pencil. Lay the graph paper on a table, and go over the design in pen, but following the straight lines of the graph paper as closely as possible to the pencil drawing. This will give you steps instead of curves, but that is characteristic of the technique.

108 *(a) The graph paper version of the seedhead.*
(b) The motif repeated to make a border pattern. This would be suitable for cross stitch or canvas work.
(c) This version is suitable for Assisi embroidery, in which the motif is outlined in double running stitch, and the background is filled in with lines of cross stitch. To make Assisi embroidery more exciting, try using lines of different coloured threads, or threads of different thicknesses or textures.
(d) This design is for Russian drawn ground. The seedhead should be outlined in heavy chain stitch and the background worked in a form of drawn thread work, in which the threads are withdrawn in pairs in both directions and covered with stitchery as in the diagram. Alternatively, the background could be of woven ribbons, or ribbons woven through fabric.

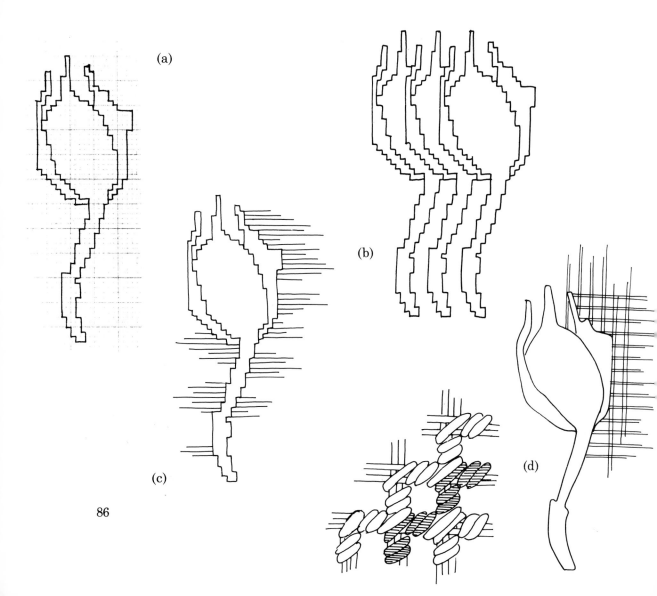

(a)

(b)

(c)

(d)

86

109 *Drawings of sliced mushrooms were stylized and simplified.*
(a) Here they were overlapped, using three different shapes.
(b) This version suggests lines of stitchery between the ribs of corduroy or between machine stitched pintucks, or lines of stitchery.

(c) In this version lines of stitchery could fill the whole design, changing colour at the edges of the shapes. It could also be a tiny or nué sample with coloured stitching over laid gold threads.
(d) This version suggests stitching in different directions, using a shiny thread to give tonal contrast.

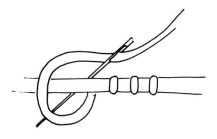

(a)

(b)

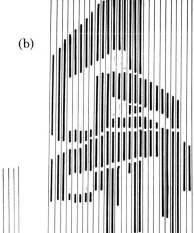

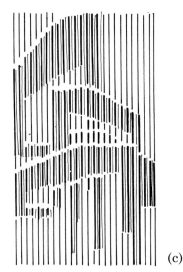

(c)

(d)

— FIVE —
DESIGNS USING NEGATIVE SHAPES

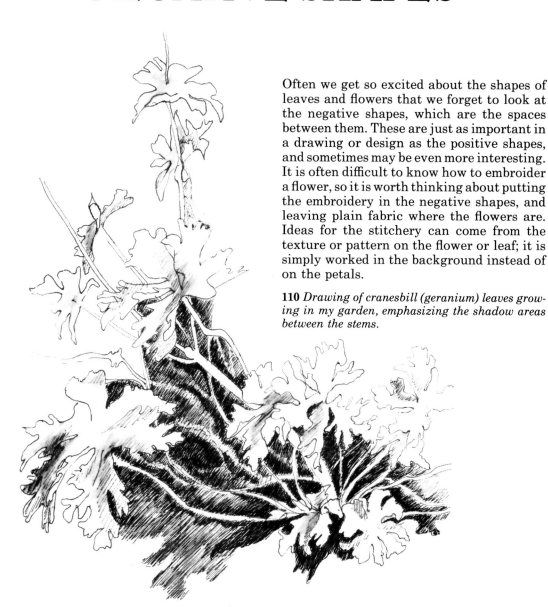

Often we get so excited about the shapes of leaves and flowers that we forget to look at the negative shapes, which are the spaces between them. These are just as important in a drawing or design as the positive shapes, and sometimes may be even more interesting. It is often difficult to know how to embroider a flower, so it is worth thinking about putting the embroidery in the negative shapes, and leaving plain fabric where the flowers are. Ideas for the stitchery can come from the texture or pattern on the flower or leaf; it is simply worked in the background instead of on the petals.

110 *Drawing of cranesbill (geranium) leaves growing in my garden, emphasizing the shadow areas between the stems.*

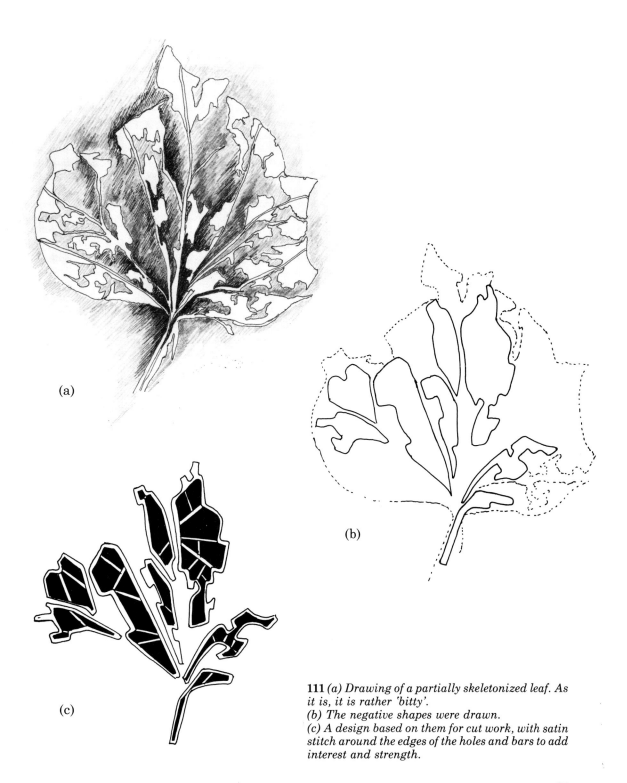

(a)

(b)

(c)

111 *(a) Drawing of a partially skeletonized leaf. As it is, it is rather 'bitty'.*
(b) The negative shapes were drawn.
(c) A design based on them for cut work, with satin stitch around the edges of the holes and bars to add interest and strength.

(a)

(b)

(c)

(d)

(e)

112 *(a) Roses and tulips. Because the rectangular edge is too far away from the flowers, the negative shapes are not particularly interesting.*
(b) The rectangular frame reduced and the negative shapes darkened.
(c) Here they are isolated to see if they could be used alone.
(d) & (e) A circular and a hexagonal frame placed behind the flowers, giving different negative shapes.

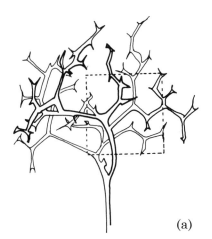

(a)

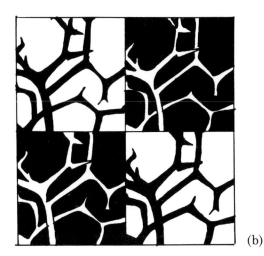

(b)

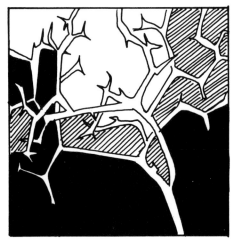

(c)

113 *A single flower repeated four times to make a pattern, placed over three squares to give negative shapes and make a much more interesting design.*

114 *(Right) (a) A window placed over part of a thorn bush to make a block design.*
(b) Four blocks used in a counterchange pattern in which the positive and negative spaces are darkened alternately.
(c) A design in which the whole bush is used and the negative spaces filled in using three tones. This suggests a book cover to me, or a box lid. I would use applied leather in the darkest and palest areas, and solid stitchery where the mid tone is.

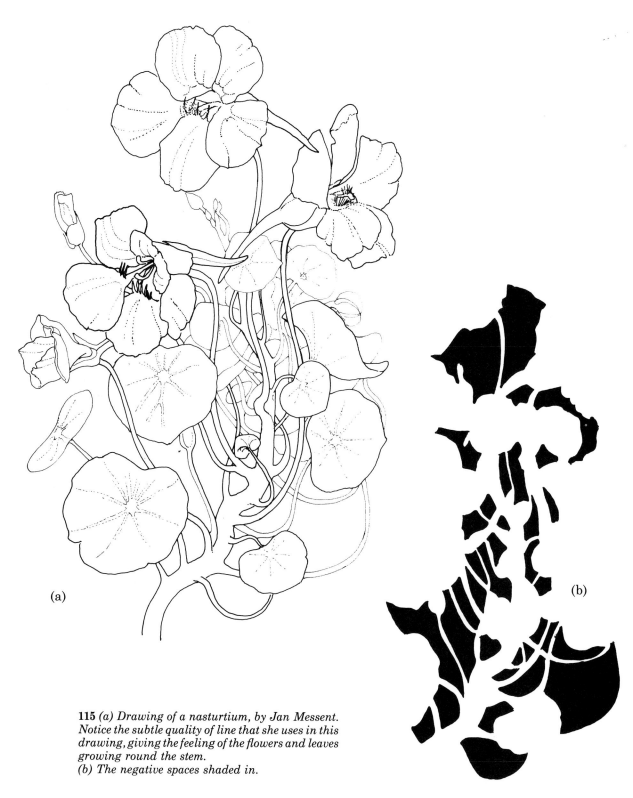

(a)

(b)

115 *(a) Drawing of a nasturtium, by Jan Messent.*
Notice the subtle quality of line that she uses in this
drawing, giving the feeling of the flowers and leaves
growing round the stem.
(b) The negative spaces shaded in.

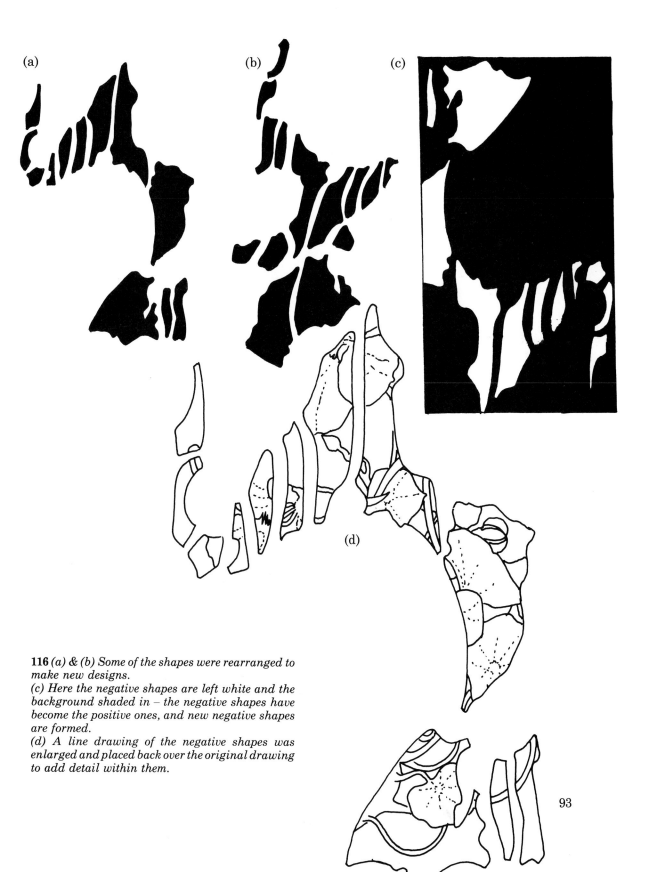

(a)

(b)

(c)

(d)

116 *(a) & (b) Some of the shapes were rearranged to make new designs.*
(c) Here the negative shapes are left white and the background shaded in – the negative shapes have become the positive ones, and new negative shapes are formed.
(d) A line drawing of the negative shapes was enlarged and placed back over the original drawing to add detail within them.

93

117 *Frost-covered grasses, with very pale tones standing out against a dark background.*

SIX

USING TONE & COLOUR

The study of colour in flowers and plants is very important to the embroiderer. It is a good idea to look at parts of a certain plant in different lighting conditions to see how the colour is affected. We also have preconceived ideas about colour – a leaf is not always just 'green'. It can be many colours, both subtle and vivid. Think of cream and green variegated leaves; the yellows, oranges, rusts, reds and browns of leaves turning colour in the autumn; or the grey-green of willows. When looking at flowers or plants, you will find that they are often in a complementary colour scheme – that is, one in which the colours are on opposite sides of the colour wheel. Think of red berries and green leaves, or purple irises with yellow stamens. Also look at the proportions of the colours in a plant or flower; they are never in equal quantities.

The colours in a single petal can suggest a colour scheme for a large embroidery, even if the embroidery is not of that flower. You can look for the following colour schemes:

1 All one colour, with varying tones, such as you might find in roses, with pale, medium and dark pinks; a cabbage, with different tones of green; or dried corn, with creams, beiges and pale dull yellows.
2 Colours that are near each other in the spectrum, such as the pinks, lilacs and blues of sweet peas; or the yellows and oranges of daisies and lilies.
3 Contrasting colours, usually complementary ones, such as the red and green of a poinsettia; or the pink and various greens with some yellow of a herbaceous border.

However, even more important than colour to make your design 'work' is tone – that is, how light or dark the colours are. Dark tones (shades) give depth to a design, bringing certain areas forward, or setting them back, according to the proportion of darks to lights. If your tones are all in the middle range, even if you have plenty of different colours, your design will look flat. It is worth drawing or painting a design in black, greys and white, as if it was a black and white photograph, to judge whether or not it is successful. Then when you decide on the colour scheme, put the dark colours where the shades are, and the pale colours where the tints are. It hardly matters what colours are used; if the tones are the same, the design will look the same. If you change the tones you will completely alter the design.

118 *Pencil drawing of chanterelle fungus, by Jan Messent. The darker tones make the most important one come forward.*

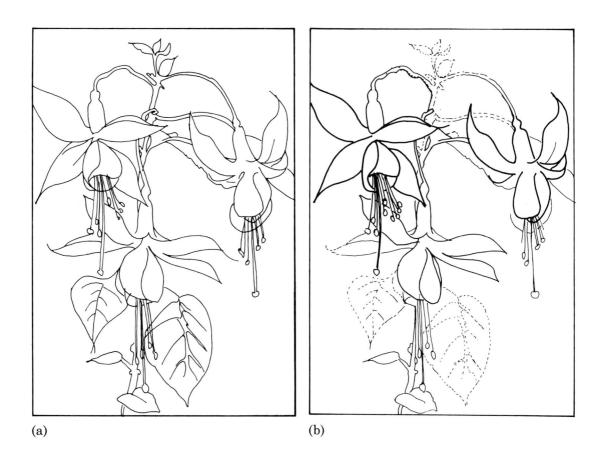

(a)   (b)

119 *(a) & (b) Two designs of fuchsias. The first one looks flat because the lines are all the same thickness; the second one has more depth because of the thick, thin and broken lines.*

(c)

(d)

120 *(c) & (d) The dark tone in the backgrounds really throws the flowers and leaves forward. This does not look so effective in black and white, but if you fill in the dark areas with a rainbow pencil (or* *streaks of different colours) it will suggest lovely rich stitchery using thick and thin threads, eyelets, lines and knots, areas of Cretan stitch in layers, loose threads and loops, and even tassels.*

(a)

(b)

121 *Usually it is the darkest tones that come forward, so you should use them to emphasize the most important parts of a design. However, there is also the matter of the proportion of the tones, and whatever is the smallest amount will come forward. So if there is a small area that is very dark, it will* *come forward, and if there is a small area of white, then that will come forward.*
(a) Here there is a conflict caused by the small black leaf which is the most important tone, and yet is right at the back, which looks all wrong.
(b) Slightly better, with the middle leaves darkened,

(c)

(d)

but still not quite 'right'.

(c) This version seems the most normal, with the most important leaf and the darkest tone being in the same place.

(d) The opposite, with a dark background and the most important leaf white. It still comes forward, because there is less of it than of the black or grey. Now you can do a colour version, using any colour scheme you like, but keeping the tones similar.

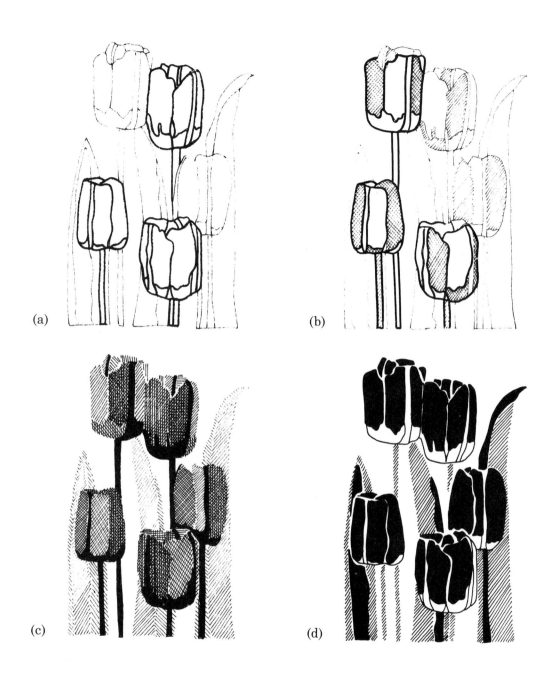

122 *A design which emphasizes the stiffness and formality of tulips.*
(a) Thicker, and therefore darker, lines come forward to place some of the tulips in front of others.
(b) Thicker lines plus areas of tone bring the tulips even further forward.

(c) Darker tones (without lines) emphasize the tulips and push the leaves into the background.
(d) Strong contrasts of tone within the flowers emphasize the interesting shapes. The original tulips were red (where the blacks are) and yellow (where the whites are) with green leaves.

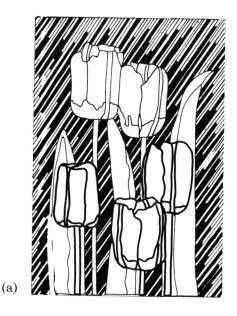

(a)

(b)

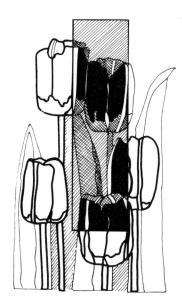

(c)

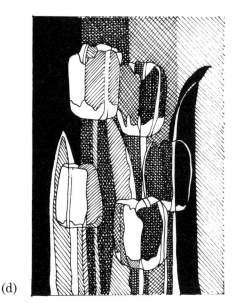

(d)

123 *(a) The diagonal lines in the background are so strong that they come forward through the flowers and leaves.*
(b) The dark areas are so near each other in tone that it is now the white areas which are emphasized, both on the flowers and leaves.
(c) A rectangle is placed over the design and the dark tones kept within that area to give it impor- *tance. This could be the embroidery and the rest of the design quilted to make a frame. Or colour could be kept within the rectangle and the same stitchery worked outside it in self-colour, again to make a frame.*
(d) The background is dark on the left-hand side and gradually gets paler; the reverse happens on the flowers and leaves.

124 *A soft panel by Dorothy Tucker, based on tulips. She has used patchwork and appliqué in silks and velvet, with blocks of straight stitches in brilliant colours to add detail. The borders hold the design together.*

125 *A velvet jacket by Dorothy Tucker, again based on tulips. She has exactly captured the stiffness and formality of tulips in log cabin and paper patch-work, with groups of tiny squares of fabric adding detail. The main body of the jacket is in dark green velvet.*

126 *An exotic piece of bark with ridges, overlapped areas and holes. This sort of texture suggests linear stitchery, also in layers, or on separate pieces of fabric which are placed on top of previous stitching.*

104

SEVEN

TEXTURE

Embroidery stitches can give an infinite variety of textures, and can be smooth, rough, fluffy, knobbly, ridged, loopy, flat or lumpy. The threads can be shiny and glossy, or rough and hairy, which can make the same stitch look completely different. The more stitchery I see, the more I think that using a contrast in the thickness of the thread is very important. Try using machine embroidery thread for the fine, open areas, and rug wool or strips of fabric for the thick areas, with plenty of different thicknesses in between. Stitching tends to even out the thickness of the thread, so choose one that is finer or thicker than you want the result to be.

The direction of stitchery is also crucial, and can make or mar a piece of work. Instead of using a different stitch, try just changing the direction. The tone changes and becomes lighter or darker as the light hits the threads at a different angle. The direction of the stitchery also carries your eye across the embroidery to another area, and provides more interest.

127 *Irises, by Irene Barnes. This tiny sample (10 × 10 cm – 4 × 4 in.) uses lock stitch in yellows and purples to depict iris flowers. The stitching is both vertical and horizontal.*

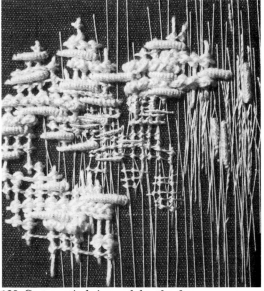

128 *Cretan stitch is used for the fine, open areas; raised chain band in fine and thick threads, and long bullion knots to give a different texture. Such stitching can represent plants in the distance.*

129 *Rubbings give a very good suggestion of texture and can suggest what stitchery to use more easily than a drawing. The irregularity is helpful when trying to work stitches more freely. Rubbings can be made with pencil or wax crayon, but I particularly like them done with a rainbow or multi-coloured pencil, and this relates to the variegated or multi-coloured threads that are available.*

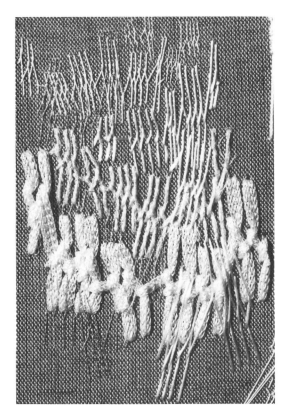

130 *Cretan stitch worked in sewing threads, crochet thread, twisted silk and shiny knitting ribbon.*

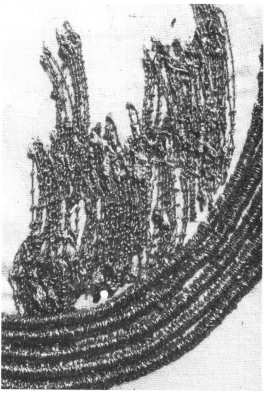

131 *A small sample of machine embroidery using whip stitch and satin stitch over string, which was worked looking closely at a rubbing.*

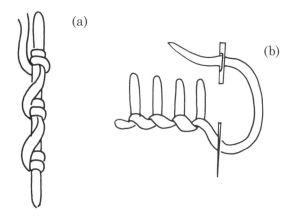

(a)

(b)

132 *(a) Portuguese knotted stem stitch, a wonderful stitch for giving a rough texture.*
(b) Blanket or buttonhole stitch. This is one of the most useful stitches in our vocabulary, and can be worked at different intervals, using stitches of different lengths, in overlapping and interlocking areas, and in layers in different directions.

133 *(Below left) Bullion knots wrongly worked, leaving long tails. Never think that because a stitch diagram in a book is drawn showing a single way of working a stitch, that it must only be worked in that way. A stitch is used to interpret an area of texture or pattern in the embroidery that you are doing, and may be varied or altered to give the effect that you want.*

134 *Needleweaving worked on long stitches, using thin, thick, matt and shiny threads. Buttonhole loops, and loops of thread, give a contrast of texture.*

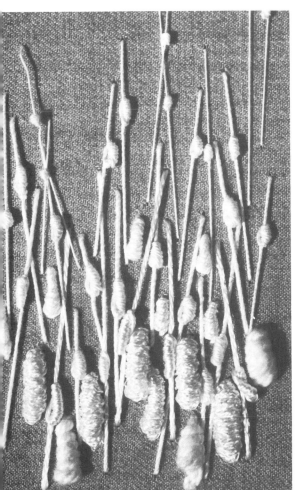

107

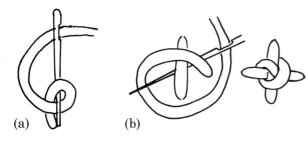

(a)   (b)

135 *(a) This is the proper way to do a French knot, with only one loop of the thread around the needle. If you want a bigger knot, then use a thicker thread. (b) Four-legged knot. An extremely useful stitch for rough textures.*

136 *(Right) Cross stitch worked freely in two directions, using thin and thick threads. Strips of fabric have wrapped some of the stitches to give a contrast.*

137 *Pulled work done with a standard, fine thread, and the same stitch using a very shiny, round cord called 'rat's tail'. Because the stitching is congested it looks rich, and the light emphasizes the different directions of the stitches.*

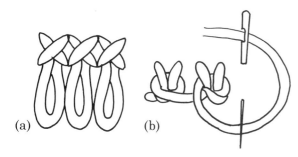

(a)   (b)

138 *(a) Velvet stitch leaves loops which can be cut or uncut as you wish, and is a good contrast to flat or knotted stitches.*
(b) German buttonhole is a less well-known version of buttonhole stitch, and can be varied beautifully.

139 *(Left) Cretan stitch using fine threads, knitting ribbon and strips cut from old nylon tights. These make an extremely good thread, and have the advantage of being free. Tights can be bleached in bleach or commercial dye remover, and then dyed with a hot (direct) dye. Then start cutting at the top of a leg and continue in a downward spiral (a helix). The thread will stretch as you use it, so cut it a bit thicker than you think it should be – anything from $\frac{1}{2}$ cm to 5 cm ($\frac{1}{4}$ in. to 2 in.) wide.*

140 *(Above) Free pulled work using fine embroidery threads, hairy knitting yarn, knitting ribbon and leather thongs.*

141 *A field of corn after the harvest. The ridges and the direction of the stalks would be lovely to interpret in stitchery.*

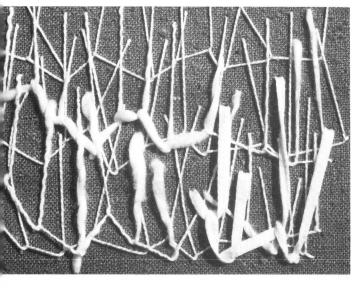

142 *Buttonhole or blanket stitch in thick, thin and slubby threads which could easily suggest corn stalks.*

143 *A sketch of part of a landscape, by Anne Hazlewood. This method of sketching can be interpreted almost directly into stitchery, or a free blackwork surface.*

144 *(Above right) Another version of Cretan stitch, wrapped with shiny knitting ribbon and strips of nylon tights.*

145 *Herringbone stitch, which is good for suggesting spiky undergrowth. Small areas of blanket or buttonhole are worked on top of some of the threads.*

146 *A design for a landscape made by gluing short lengths of noodles and spaghetti, rice, seeds, pasta rings and barley to a thick piece of card, partially covered with thin strips of torn paper to suggest the sky. When the glue was dry, the whole thing was sprayed with car spray paint. This could be interpreted using rich stitchery such as French knots, bullion knots, detached chain using a thick thread, straight stitches and raised chain band, with torn and frayed strips of fabric for the sky. Alternatively it could be carried out in fabric only (see fig. 148).*

147 *Wave stitch, using ribbon, rayon floss, knitting ribbon, crochet cotton, and a slub knitting yarn. The contrast of matt and shiny is important, as is the contrast in size of thread. Parts of the stitching have needleweaving worked over them to give added texture.*

112

148 *A panel worked by Jennie Parry, based on a river. The river is worked in fine stitchery over and under transparent fabric. The banks are entirely of calico, manipulated in various ways to suggest plants and stones. Areas of gathering and ruching,* *rolled folded strips, frayed strips sewn closely, Suffolk puffs, small stuffed balls, and folded shapes contrast with areas of stitchery in cream. When as much texture as this is used, the colour scheme must be extremely limited, otherwise confusion follows.*

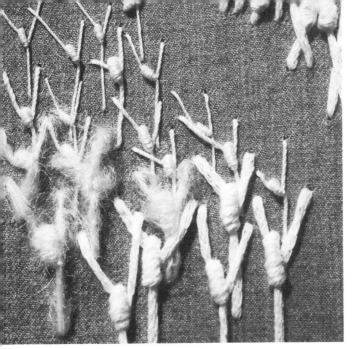

149 *Fly stitch combined with bullion knots suggests spiky, upward-thrusting growth.*

150 *Dead bracken. Using photographs of texture such as this can help to free your stitchery. Follow it as closely as possible, keeping the change of size and direction, the contrast between the long stems and the curled, untidy fronds, and the variation in density. In my experience, the more closely you follow the original, the more exciting the stitching will be.*

151 *A detail of canvas work using tent and straight stitches, fly stitch, knotted lengths of knitting ribbons, back-stitched wheels and needlewoven bars. Many stitches, other than the conventional ones, can be used in canvas work.*

152 *A sponge painting of a path through a garden. I used thick white paint, and small pieces of sponge sometimes dabbed or dragged, and with varying pressure, to build up the picture. It suggests canvas work to me, but could also be carried out in hand or machine surface stitchery.*

153 *A bag by Doreen Bibby. It is based on a quick, impressionistic painting of part of a garden, and worked in the greens, reds and pinks of the garden. The shape arose from part of an Elizabethan knot garden, and the three small bags fit inside the large one.*

154 *(Opposite) A detail of the stitchery. Satin stitch and straight stitching were first worked on a small piece of 16s. canvas. This was applied to a piece of fabric and further stitching worked through both layers. Then loops were worked using the tailor tacking or looping foot, and knots of ribbon added. There is no hand stitchery at all, and the texture of the solid machining is very rich.*

The edges of the bag were bound, and ribbon handles and tassel added. The lining is quilted.

EIGHT

THE FINISHED EMBROIDERY

The difficulty of translating a design on paper into an embroidery can be daunting, and needs a great deal of thought. A finished piece does not usually leap into the mind's eye, but needs working towards – often doing more than one drawing or design, perhaps in different media to suggest different interpretations. The next stage is to think of the shape of the finished embroidery. Is it to be a wall-hanging, a quilt, a book cover, a blind, or a bag? The finished piece will also determine to a large extent the method and type of embroidery, and the sort of fabrics and threads you can use.

Quite a few trials and experiments may be needed to discover the results of stitchery in different threads on different fabrics, perhaps trying out colour combinations that are new to you, and working out new ways of interpreting your ideas about the design. Most people skimp this stage, as they are anxious to start on the final piece. However, the more samples and experiments you do before starting, the quicker and more spontaneous the result will be, as you will have more idea of where you are going and what effects you like.

Writing down words while you are working on the design helps spark the imagination, and these words should be evocative of the original subject. They should describe the atmosphere, mood or style; the textures; the quality of light and shade; and also the different qualities such as fragility or strength, movement or stillness. Most people work too quickly, with too little thought, and then get stuck in the middle of the embroidery. More time and thought spent at the beginning cuts down the time actually spent doing the piece, and so avoids the possibility of boredom.

WHAT TO DO WITH A MOTIF OR DRAWING OR PHOTOGRAPHS

Many people are inspired by a tree, a flower or a small section of a garden, but really have no idea of what to do next. The next few pages offer some suggestions which you can try the next time you are in that situation.

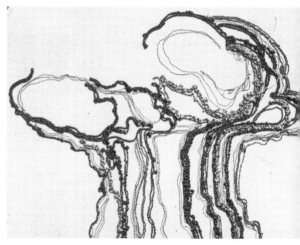

155 *A machine embroidered tree, using free running and cable stitch. It is slightly abstracted but still gives the essence of the tree, the lines on the trunks and the bulbous shapes of the top.*

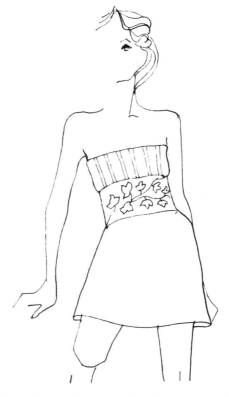

156 *Sketches by Deborah Post showing how a spray of leaves can be used on clothes. The placing dictates the method that will be used for the embroidery. While the leaves on the shoulder of the jacket can be* thick and quilted to give a broad-shouldered look, on the midriff of the dress they should be flat and should not crease too much when worn.

USING A MOTIF

1 First of all draw or trace it, or photocopy it, so that you have something flat, of a reasonable size, to work with.

2 Enlarge or reduce it on a photocopier, or use the grid method. The size may have been wrong in the first place, or you might wish to use different sizes in the same design.

3 Cut a stencil (a hole) and a template (a shape) from a piece of thin card. You can spray through or over these, or draw round them a number of times to build up patterns. The sprayed shapes can be used as a background to the linear ones, both on the paper design and on the fabric before starting the embroidery.

4 Using the template, cut a number of silhouettes from paper and glue them to another paper, which can be patterned or textured. For example, silhouettes of plants can be glued to an illustration of a garden, taken from a magazine.

5 Design repeat patterns using two, three, four or more motifs facing different ways. Look for the patterns and shapes that occur between the motifs – these are the negative shapes and can often be even more interesting.

6 Draw or trace mirror images of the motifs, photocopy them to give you a number to work with, and then use them to build up bands and borders. Add extra lines or patterns to add richness. Many bands next to each other can make an all-over design.

7 Make a collage of repeats of your motif, using cut, torn or burnt edges if they help the design. This is a quick way of working out a design, and plain, patterned, transparent and textured papers can be used.

8 Cut a design into strips and spread them out. Re-join some of the lines between the strips to connect them up, thinking of working these in stitchery.

9 Cut a photograph or illustration into

119

10 Make or cut a printing block from your motif. Either cut card shapes and glue them to another piece of card, or glue string to a piece of card. Blocks can also be cut from lino, potatoes or finely textured polystyrene. Paint fabric paint on to the block with a household brush and press on to the fabric. Iron it to set the colour. Embroidery can be worked on top, or the fabric can be pleated or gathered to distort the pattern, and then stitched or smocked.

11 Overlap shapes to make patterns, or to make a new shape. Use one shape and repeat it a number of times, or use two or three similar shapes together.

12 Design a counterchange pattern. Place a motif inside a square, and divide it into four. Colour it in, using two contrasting colours, and filling in the shapes alternately. Where the background in one square is colour *a*, in the next square the motif will be that colour. Fill all the squares like this.

13 Isolate small areas of details of a larger photograph, drawing or design, and use them on their own. The easiest way to do this is to cut four strips of paper and place them on the drawing, making a frame for whatever detail you want. This can then be enlarged on the photocopier to give you a new design.

14 Place your motif inside a square, oval or circle so that it touches all the edges. You might have to adapt the motif somewhat so that it fits well, and looks satisfactory. Use it on its own, or repeat it to make a different pattern.

15 Trace three or five motifs on to tracing paper, making a good arrangement of them. Place the tracing over a single geometric shape (a rectangle, perhaps) which is smaller than the outside shape of the tracing. Colour in the background areas up to the edge of the geometric shape, but not the motifs.

Many of these have been tried out in other chapters of the book, but it is useful to have this list for the times you are stumped and cannot think what to do.

157 A small panel by Isobel Elliot, worked in couched gold on marbled fabric. In some places the gold has been stitched with coloured threads.

strips, and weave it with plain coloured strips, or strips cut from another illustration, going in the opposite direction. Choose a small area of this and draw it in coloured pencils, with all your pencil strokes going in one direction. Enlarge it and you will have a design based on a square grid with some plain areas to contrast with the patterned ones.

1 A bag, with three tiny ones which fit inside it. The
base is machine embroidery on canvas, which is applied
to fabric and further machining worked over both fabrics.
(Doreen Bibby)

2 A waterfall, mainly in machine embroidery, with fabric and polythene. *(Ewa Kuniczak-Coles)*

3 'Poppies'. Frayed edges and irregular folds suggest the fragility of the flowers. *(Yvonne Morton)*

4 A garden, worked in hand stitchery on painted fabric, net and transparent fabrics. *(Julia Barton)*

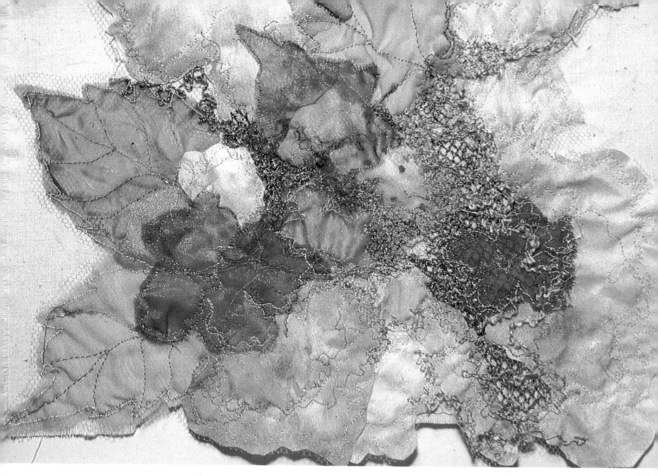

5 'Leaves'. Painted transparent fabrics with machine embroidery and some scattered beads. *(Julia Barton)*

6 A tiny embroidery of irises, completely worked in lock stitch. *(Irene Barnes)*

7 'Wild Flower Garden'. Painting and machine embroidery within a painted frame.
(Verina Warren)

8 Machine embroidered landscape with a shaggy frame of fabric strips and loops.
(Phyl Gunstone)

9 A flower bag made by machine stitching on water soluble fabric. *(Jan Beaney)*

10 *(Below left)* A daisy bag, also made by machining on soluble fabric, with a silver lining. *(Jan Beaney)*

11 *(Below)* Two cushions, from a drawing of a spider plant. Machine and hand stitchery with appliqué. *(Marian Murphy)*

12 *(Above)* 'A Winter Garden'. A large panel with machine embroidery on fabrics, plastics and papers; machine-made lace; and sprayed gathered fabric. *(Chris Cooke)*

13 Detail of 'A Winter Garden', showing embroidery, nets, lace leaves, skeletonized leaves and dried hydrangea petals. *(Chris Cooke)*

158 *An iris, by Wendy Williams. Each petal has been stitched and quilted, and made up into a very real-looking flower.*

159 *A flower cushion, by Jane Lemon. The velvet leaves were sprayed through a stencil, to give the vein lines, then stitched and quilted. The flower has appliqué shapes and lines of stitching, with loops at the centre.*

160 *A page from a 'Garden Book', by Julia Barton. The fabric was painted and then quilted, with added surface stitchery. The arch in the wall makes a frame for the garden seen through it.*

161 (Opposite) *Designing from a photograph usually works well, as it is already two-dimensional. This one was taken of frosted leaves in my daughter's garden.*

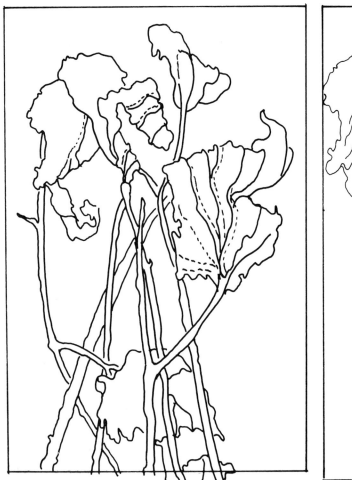 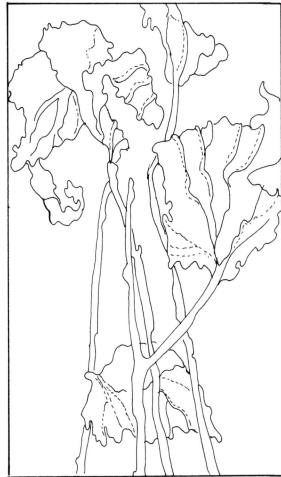

162 *(a) First make a photocopy of the photograph, to avoid spoiling the original. Then trace it. Leave out some of the detail to simplify it.*

(b) A tracing of fig. 161, leaving out some of the stems, and bringing in the frame to make a better composition.

(c) Another tracing, with some shapes filled in with black to give a strong focal point. These could be interpreted in appliqué or solid stitchery. The rest of the leaves and stems could be couching or stitchery, and the background filled in with diagonal lines of fine stitchery or quilting.

(d) Another tracing using lines to indicate stitchery, appliqué or stuffed areas. The background was originally done in a rainbow pencil and could be worked in hand or machine stitchery, lines of cords or rouleaux, or gold threads couched in colour in the shadow areas (or nué). The next stage is to do samples in threads and fabric.

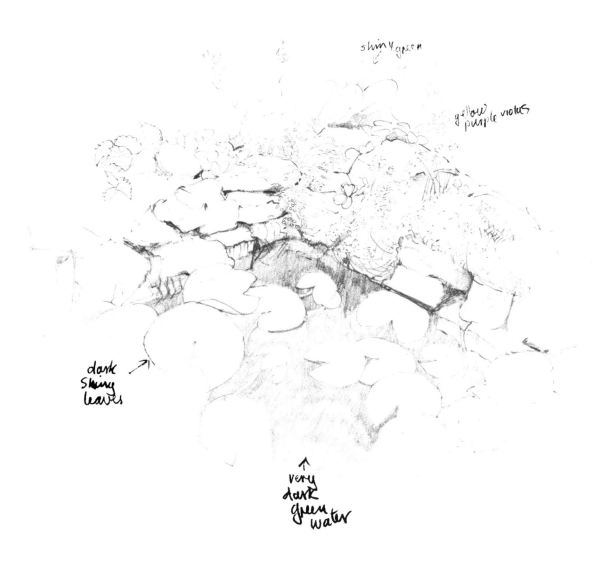

shiny green

yellow purple violets

dark shiny leaves

very dark green water

163 *A drawing by Christine Cooke of part of a water garden. She draws in a way that is very helpful to her embroidery, as it suggests different textures which can easily be translated into fine stitchery. Her notes are also a useful reminder when she comes back to the design.*

164 (Opposite) *An embroidery of a wood by Muriel Best, worked on pink evenweave fabric in dark blues and greens. The buttonhole shapes make a good contrast to the straight stitching, and the empty spaces are important to the design.*

165 *Drawings by Mary Youles of details from a dried ear of corn, with suggestions for areas to isolate for embroidery. These areas can be square, rectangular, triangular, circular or oval shapes. When enlarged they make good compositions or designs for wall panels or hangings, box tops, patterns on clothes, or book covers. The dark areas can be the focal point, or centre of interest.*

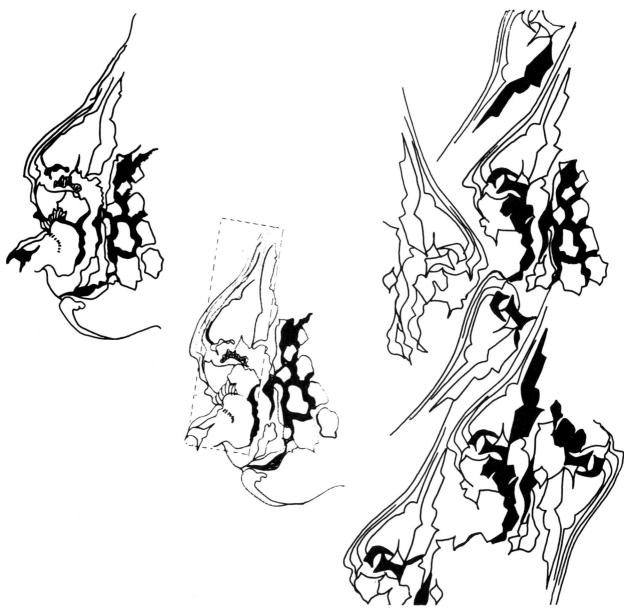

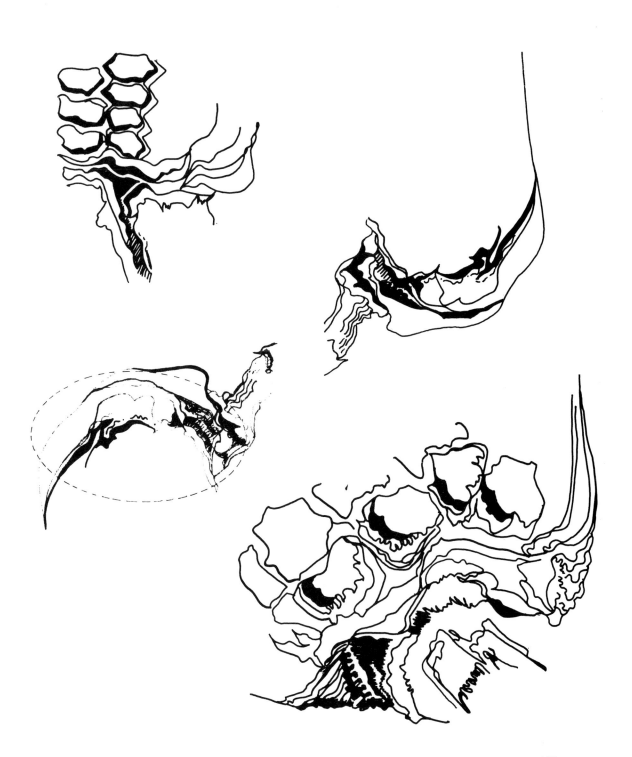

129

166 *A drawing from a photograph of mushrooms growing in compost. The different sizes of the mushrooms give depth and a feeling of recession to the design, and this should be enhanced by a change in the size of the stitches.*

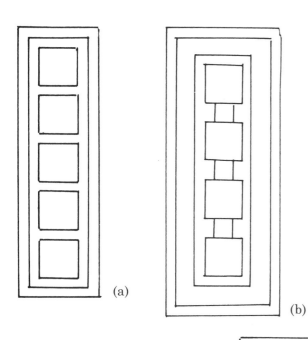

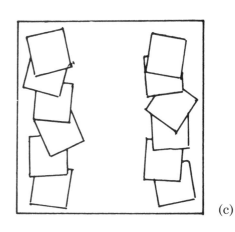

(a)

(b)

(c)

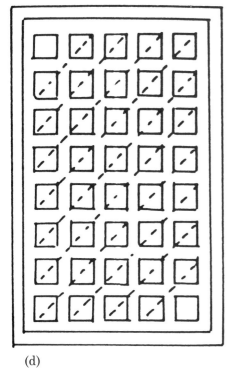

(d)

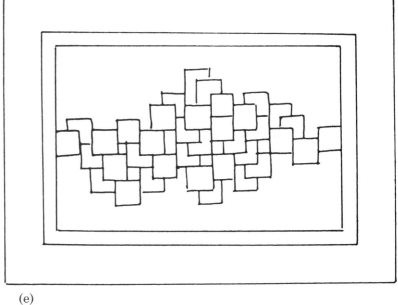

(e)

167 *(a) to (e) Some suggestions for layouts using individual motifs, repeated, or square isolated details of a larger drawing. When the same is repeated as in these layouts, a gradual change of colour can be introduced. The diagonal lines on (d) suggest diagonal bands of colour.*

Fence

168 *A pencil drawing by Christine Cooke of part of a garden. This is a more informal composition than* fig. 163. *Here, the empty spaces are as important as the ones with detail.*

169 *'Spring Woods', by Jean Mould, from a sketch made at Hawkwood College, Stroud. She did some pencil drawing on vilene, then black machine embroidery for nearly all the panel, except for the blossom, which is in white whip stitch.*

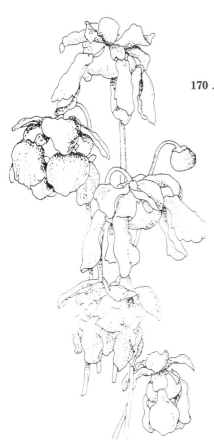

170 *A spray of exotic flowers.*

171 *They were traced several times and coloured in with felt pens. Very fine black lines were drawn over all the shapes in different directions to give a feeling of unity and a sense of direction. Shapes were cut from the drawing and glued to another sheet of paper, together with plain coloured paper.*

172 *A stencil of a bag was cut in black paper and laid over the collage. A stencil of a garment could also have been used.*

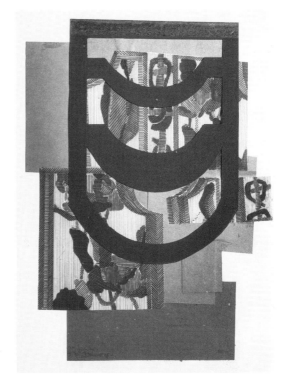

173 *One of the samples worked using this design, with pink stranded cotton used singly in different directions to give changes of tone, between areas of padding.*

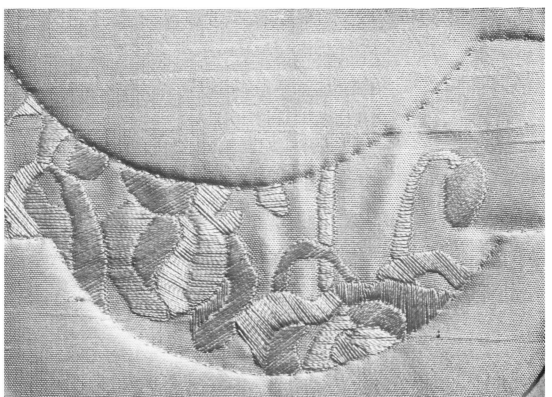

174 *'Summer', by Dorothy Tucker. Pieced squares of silk fabric stitched on to silk. The whole was then quilted and stitched. The colours and texture give a joyful feeling of high summer, while not being at all literal.*

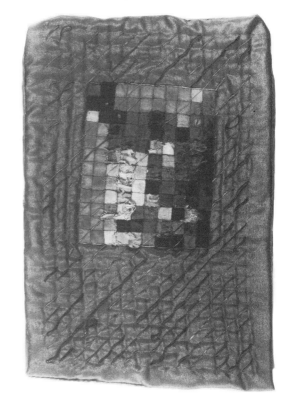

175 *(Below) A tiny garden worked in machine cross stitch on canvas, with hand-worked cross stitches over the top. The border is of thick loops, worked on the machine using the tailor tacking or looping foot.*

176 *Another abstract garden by Eunice Wells, with woven strips of space dyed fabric, added French knots and straight stitches.*

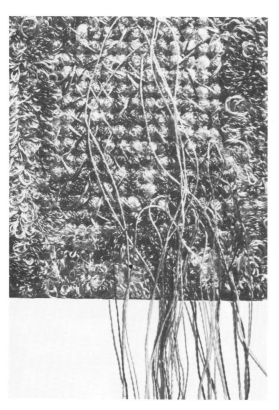

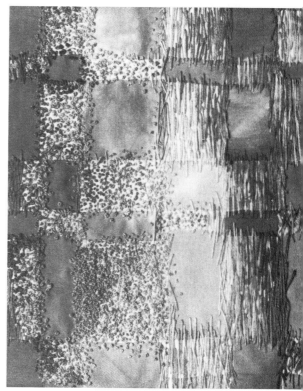

177 *'Tulips', by Dorothy Tucker. Fine silk and cotton threads stitched into evenweave fabric. The distinguishing feature of this panel is that the flowers in the foreground and middle ground are in colour, while the factory and smoke in the background are grey.*

178 *Plants in pots, drawn by Christine Cooke. A beautifully sensitive drawing of delicate flower petals, with darker background tone emphasizing them.*

179 *A panel by Wendy Williams. The arch is padded over stiff card, with stuffed areas and lines of string around the curved edge. The garden is sprayed, with added hand and machine embroidery, padded areas, three-dimensional quilted leaves, fabric manipulation, organza leaves and wrapped threads. The whole panel is of calico.*

180 (*Opposite*) *An etching, by my daughter Sarah Brownie. It shows a view of a landscape through a gap in ivy leaves. This is a good way of framing an exquisite, tiny embroidery, with fabric and stitched leaves.*

181 *Garden box, by Jane Lemon. Some painting on fabric, appliqué, needleweaving, crochet, loops and knots give the rich texture of a garden.*

FURTHER READING

Bager, Bertel, *Nature as Designer*, Frederick Warne

Beaney, Jan, *Stitches: New Approaches*, Batsford

Bruandet, Pierre, *Introducing Photograms*, Batsford

Butler, Anne, *Batsford Encyclopaedia of Embroidery Stitches*, Batsford

Harlow, William, *Art Forms from Plant Life*, Dover

Kaden, Vera, *The Illustration of Plants and Gardens 1500–1850*, Victoria and Albert Museum

King, Ronald, *Botanical Illustration*, Ash & Grant

Marein, Shirley, *Flowers in Design*, David & Charles

Mathew, Brian, *The Iris*, Batsford

Messent, Jan, *Embroidery and Nature*, Batsford

Practical Study Group of the Embroiderers' Guild, *Needlework School*, Windward

Putnam, Clare, *Flowers and Plants of Tudor England*, Hugh Evelyn

Readers' Digest Guide to Creative Gardening, Readers' Digest Association

Stevens, Peter S., *Patterns in Nature*, Penguin

SUPPLIERS

Please write to any of the following firms and ask for a price list, to check what they are currently supplying, as this changes from time to time.

Borovicks
16 Berwick Street
London W1
Wide range of fabrics, including transparent ones

Campden Needlecraft Centre
High Street
Chipping Campden
Gloucestershire
Wide range of embroidery supplies

Creative Beadcraft Ltd
Unit 26
Chiltern Trading Estate
Holmer Green
High Wycombe
Bucks
Beads

Crown Needlework
High Street
Hungerford
Berkshire
General embroidery supplies

Eastern Delights
2 Pine Close
High Street
Everton
Doncaster
South Yorkshire
Indian silk fabrics

Liberty & Co.
Regent Street
London W1
Fabrics, unusual knitting yarns

MacCulloch & Wallis
25–26 Dering Street
London W1R 0BH
Fabrics, haberdashery

Mace & Nairn
89 Crane Street
Salisbury
Wiltshire
General embroidery supplies

John P. Milner Ltd
Cilycwm
Llandovery
Dyfed SA20 0SS
Gloving leathers

Pongees Ltd
184–6 Old Street
London EC1V 9BP
Silk fabrics, large quantities only

Christine Riley
53 Barclay Street
Stonehaven
Kincardineshire AB3 2AR
General embroidery supplies

Shades
57 Candlemas Lane
Beaconsfield
Buckinghamshire HP9 1AE
Unusual and difficult to find items

Silken Strands
33 Linksway
Gatley
Cheadle
Cheshire SK8 4LA
Threads, beads. Mail order only

Silverknit
Park Road
Calverton
Nottingham NG14 6LL
Yarns, fine gold & silver thread

Terry Taylor Associates
27 Woodland Road
Tunbridge Wells
Kent TN4 9HW
Fabric paints, silk fabrics

Thomas Thorp
170 High Street
Guildford
Surrey GU1 3HP
Publishers' remainders, including art & craft books

George Weil & Sons Ltd
63–65 Riding House Street
London W1P 7PP
Silk & cotton fabrics, fabric paints

Whaleys (Bradford) Ltd
Harris Court
Great Horton
Bradford
West Yorkshire BD7 4EQ
Fabrics

H. Wolfin & Son
64 Great Tichfield Street
London W1P 7AE
Fabrics

INDEX